Pathological Positivity

The Proven Positivity Formula For:
Personal Development
Parenting
Relationships

Paul H. Jenkins, Ph.D.

PAUL H. JENKINS, PH.D.

LIVE ON PURPOSE

By the time you finish this book, you will be living the life you love, on purpose, with

Pathological Positivity

The practices for personal power contained in this book shift your fundamental perception. All problems, from the mildest disappointment to the greatest tragedies, will no longer appear as problems but as opportunities – or "propportunities!"

The greater the problem, the greater the opportunity for greatness.

You will know that whatever happens *to* you is *for* you. Regardless of your circumstances, you will move forward and create the life you love.

Dr. Paul Jenkins works with organizations and individuals to establish and maintain habitual patterns of positive perception and focus which increase happiness, engagement, productivity, profit, and ultimate achievement of professional and personal life missions.

DrPaulJenkins.com

Praise for *Pathological Positivity*...

"We should all be 'Pathologically Positive.' Dr. Paul Jenkins has distilled the essence of his cutting edge yet practical philosophy into this book. He will challenge you, provoke you, provide fresh insights and get you to re-think how you deal with life."

~ **Mark Sanborn**, bestselling author of The *Fred Factor, You Don't Need a Title to be a Leader* and *The Encore Effect.*

"Pathological Positivity" will make a difference in your life. This is a must read for anyone who wants to overcome disappointments and achieve their dreams."

~ **Chad Hymas**, international speaker and best-selling author

"Dr. Paul's Pathological Positivity is right on the mark! Engaging, informative, filled with real life experiences from his years of results-oriented practice!"

~ **Jon Gordon**, best-selling author of *The Energy Bus, The Positive Dog,* and *The Seed*

"Dr. Paul helps you find simple solutions to complex problems and inspires the best results for your life. *Pathological Positivity* brings clarity to why you do what you do and how to change those habits that hold you back. It will turn your life around."

~ **Woody Woodward**, Author, *Your Emotional Fingerprint*

"Pathological Positivity paints a clear picture of our power to choose our happiness and break free from negative choices. Paul's gentle humor brings a sense of a kitchen table chat as well as professional one-on-one therapy to live a more purposeful life. This book is a 'must-read'!"

~ **Pam Hansen**, author of *Running with Angels*

"Pathological Positivity is uplifting, motivating—and realistic. You discover simple principles that form a *mindset* that makes something more of your life. Act, achieve and know real success with these principles!"
~ **Rich Christiansen**, USA-Today, bestselling author of *The Zigzag Principle* and *Bootstrap Business*

"Pathological Positivity isn't 'insane' it's 'unsane' – and, sure as God made little green apples, it works – oh yes, how it works (in the boardroom, the courtroom, and the schoolroom). Through intentional, repeated practice of *Pathological Positivity*, a new language is formed, new mental and emotional defaults are set, one's conditioned response to life's constant challenges becomes habitually hopeful and constructive."
~ **Thomas Cantrell**, Administrative Law Advocates, International

Foreword

All you need is love.
Why?
The Feeling.

I want to get rich.
Why?
The Feeling.

Can I take your order?
I'll take a burger and curly fries.
Why?
The Feeling.

What is your quest?
I seek the Holy Grail.
Why?
The Feeling.

We are all after one thing: *The Feeling. The Feeling* that life is good. *The Feeling* that life is great. That life is perfect. This is our quest. All theories, philosophies, policies, practices and tools are roads which are intended to lead us to that Rome – to feel good, better, great.

Success is accomplished through an accurate understanding and application of what brings us *The Feeling.*

Failure is accomplished through an erroneous understanding and application of what brings us *The Feeling.*

Our objective in life is to achieve or acquire *The Feeling. Pathological Positivity* is the process for acquiring *The Feeling.* It always works!

Pathological? Doesn't "pathological" mean insane?

In psychological lingo, "pathological" generally means crazy or disordered – disconnected from reality. It can also mean compulsively driven, as in "pathological liar."

A pathological liar says things everyone knows cannot possibly be true — *and they should know it too!*

With *Pathological Positivity,* we doggedly insist on a way of thinking that brings *The Feeling* regardless of our circumstances. We live on purpose through the powerful science of *Pathological Positivity,* regardless of how crazy it might seem.

Author's Note For The Second Edition

Since the release of the first edition in 2014, the principles in this book have been condensed into a tight model for positivity summarized now in my mini-book, *Portable Positivity* (there's a dot-com for that title). As a companion to this volume, *Portable Positivity* will give you a pocket-sized reference to power up your personal development, parenting, relationships.

This second edition features a new cover design and some corrections and edits I discovered while reading the book to you (available through Audible).

I am continually humbled and immensely pleased by the outpouring of gratitude from readers, audiences, and our YouTube followers (Live On Purpose TV) expressing how powerful these principles have been in transforming their lives and key relationships. Engage with our community and reach out to share your story as well. I would love to hear from you about your positivity story — Paul@DrPaulJenkins.com.

TABLE OF CONTENTS

Part One: Pathologically Positive Evaluation

1   Lightning Strikes   1
    Stuck in the Muck

2   The Problem Isn't Really the Problem   9
    The Power of Discontent

3   The Feeling   17
    Illuminating the Obvious

4   Metacognition   23
    What Are You Thinking

5   Compared to What?   27
    Coulda' Woulda' Shoulda' Works Both Ways

6   Power Tools   39
    Plug This In and Give Er' a Whirl

7   Posiception   45
    The Power of Positive Perception

8   The Choice   53
    Victim or Agent

9   The Power of Choice   73
    Kleenex and Concentration Camps

10 Propportunity   83
    Houston, We Have a Problem

11 The Pollyanna Proposal   91
    Corporate Croutons

12 Surprise!   99
    The Predictability of Principle

Part Two: Pathologically Positive Creation

13 The Creation of Creation   107
    Assignment of Meaning

14 Power of Principle   115
    The Trouble with Technique

15 So to Speak   123
    Change Your Language, Change Your Life

16 Wreckers or Builders   135
    The Power of Positive Planning

17 Dreaming and Scheming   149
    Plan Your Work and Work Your Plan – It Works

18 The Power of Practice   159
    From Fault to a New Default

19 The Power of Work   169
    The Means to the Miracle

20 Pain Pushes, Pleasure Pulls   175
    Either Way, We Move

21 Your Human Treasury   185
    Nobody Gets Out of This Alive

22 Life is a Game   197
    Let's Play

23 Do It Now   203
    There is No Time But the Present

24 Live On Purpose   209
    Create and Live the Life You Love

    ℞ Pathological Positivity Prescription ℞   215

    Acknowledgements   221

    Bibliography   223

    About the Author   227

Part One

Pathologically Positive Evaluation

PAUL H. JENKINS, PH.D.

Chapter One

Lightning Strikes
Stuck in the Muck

It happens.
~ Forrest Gump

The solid black mass of clouds arching overhead is a giant umbrella trimmed in glowing cobalt. The sky rumbles in the distance like an awakening lion. Patches of fluorescent blue light dance on the edges of this dramatically dark morning sky. I feel the impending power of an intense summer thunderstorm.

When the sky breaks loose in the high Utah mountain desert, watch out – or better yet, go out and watch it! I hurry to my daughter's room and gently awaken her. My sweet Lyndi loves lightning storms as much as I do. She will certainly want to see this!

The rumblings come closer, grow louder. The air heaves and sighs as a living thing. Brilliant flashes take quick snapshots of our cul-de-sac as if to document what the world is before it explodes.

Is that feeling on my skin excess electricity in the air or anticipation? One Mississippi, two Mississippi, three…

Boom!

Vicki, my wonderful, loyal wife of twenty-six years, joins us on the porch sleepily squinting into the dark morning, slightly miffed that I didn't wake her too. Who can sleep through this fireworks display? Who would want to? Astraphobics run for cover or cower in corners when lightning threatens. Our family, however, embraces this kind of experience and talks about it for days.

Blinding light rips a jagged tear through the morning sky, followed in a fraction of a second by a deafening crack. Heavy echoing reverberations remind us of how small we are. I pull my girls close. Hard rain pummels the pavement. The missing downspout on our neighbor's rain gutter becomes Yosemite Falls. We huddle together, awed by nature's display of discontent.

Discontent. A disturbance in the atmosphere. An imbalance seeking equilibrium.

Lightning is an electrostatic discharge resulting from an electric imbalance in the atmosphere. When a positive charge develops in one area and a negative one in another, nature restores the balance with a small zap of static electricity or a huge rolling thunderous blast, depending on how much imbalance has built up.

Those of you who are married know what I mean.

Discontent is a natural part of life. It is the first step in the process of creation. This feeling; that something is out of balance, out of place, missing, or incomplete; known as discontent, drives everything we do.

My mind carries me back to an earlier negative charge that built up in my world, resulting in a thunderous blast which left me cowering in the corner.

Six years earlier at three o'clock on a cool, clear morning in early summer. Vicki and I herd four bleary-eyed teenagers into our over-stacked, tightly-packed Dodge Caravan for our annual trek to the Pacific Northwest.

Vicki rides shotgun. She sits right next to me to be sure I stay awake. The kids crawl over each other into the back of the minivan, and curl into their blankets and pillows. They can shorten this seventeen hour marathon drive by being unconscious for most of it. They've brought a stack of DVDs that they can dig into somewhere in Idaho, when unconsciousness releases its merciful hold on them.

I am a morning person. Vicki definitely is not. She hangs in with me until we hit the freeway. After multiple reassurances that I am wide awake and it's safe for me to drive, she puts in her earplugs and tries to get as much sleep as she can before the second driving shift.

Our midnight blue minivan slips silently through early morning darkness, I am alone now, the only conscious soul in a graveyard of tangled sleeping bodies.

My feelings grow darker. It is not darkest before the dawn. It is darkest in the middle of the night, at the bottom of a well, with one's head wrapped in a blanket, after a severe beating. Someone sighs deeply. It's me. It sounds like a groan of despair. I'm grateful no one is awake to hear that.

Usually, I'm excited to get away to the beautiful state of Washington. I eagerly anticipate our adventures in the Northwest – the crisp clean smell of rain; the dark sweet taste of giant blackberries; invigorating moist coastal air in the lush forested Cascade Mountains.

This year, however, Vicki and I are stuck in the muck. In the past year and a half we have experienced a precipitous drop from a busy two hundred dollar-an-hour psychology practice with great investments in real estate and other high-end assets, to…

…disaster.

My client base is cut in half. Investments have gone sour. We are left with giant liabilities and payments I have no idea how to meet without the investment income. Life has struck with a thunderous blast. We are reeling from the blow.

It is easy to be positive when it is light and people are paying me for my wise counsel, but in these honesty-provoking wee hours of the morning, amid the droning monotony of tires on cool early morning pavement, my mental mainframe is processing like it's pathologically possessed.

We have made this trip every year since before Lyndi, now twelve, was born. Even though we can ill afford it, we are still going. We are not about to give in to our woes and worries at the expense of this wonderful family tradition.

This time, though, it feels more like a pathetic pilgrimage than a lighthearted vacation.

When our three boys were little, our biggest challenge was to keep them occupied during the long ride. Now we have a different problem – getting them into the van in the first place! Brennan is now fifteen years old. Adam is seventeen. Ryan, nineteen. I watch the boys fold their long legs into the back seats of the van. Lyndi curls into whatever vacant space she can find.

This should be fun. It's not. I feel an overwhelming mixture of fear, worry, defeat. By now, we should be set. By now, we should have plenty put away towards college for the kids, but we don't. I can't even think about retirement. Vicki and I have the best marriage I know of, but I feel her worry, her disappointment. That hurts. Zap!

I am filled with shame, guilt, defeat as I anticipate seeing Vicki's father later today. Two decades ago, when I married Vicki, I promised him I would take good care of his daughter. What will I say to him now? Zing!

As much as I wanted to leave them behind, I packed up my fear and worry right along with the extra socks. Excess baggage of guilt and shame are coming with me.

Maybe getting away to another state will get me into a better state of mind.

Early in the morning, when the world is still asleep, is my time. This is my golden time for study, writing, thought. I wrote most of my doctoral dissertation before seven o'clock in the morning. It is a way of life that has always served me well. Perhaps it will serve me again today.

> The heights by great men reached and kept,
> Were not attained by sudden flight

But they, while their companions slept,
Were toiling upward in the night.[1]

I plug in my stereo headphones and call on George Clason for help. His insightful story, *The Richest Man in Babylon,* has been waiting in my stack of audio books for just this moment of financial and emotional crisis. It now leaps forward to assist me.

The family is asleep. It is just me, the road, and George. I drive. Listen. Think. Process. The sonorous voice of the professional narrator intones, "A part of all you earn is yours to keep."

A part? I'll be lucky to have *anything* to keep – including my sanity. Mine to keep? For decades, that has been the theme song of positive attitude gurus and practical financial advisors alike. It is a tune, however, to which I have not faithfully danced– and now it seems the dance is over. We saved a little here and there, but never really disciplined ourselves to consistently put away a portion of everything that came in.

Discipline? Financial discipline, emotional discipline, mental discipline. Prepare for the tough times, so the tough times don't come – and if they do they will be a heck of a lot easier to handle.

I think to myself, "Yes. This makes great sense. I'll do better. I'll create better habits. I'll be a better husband, dad, provider, friend, counselor." Maybe this financial crisis will help me have more empathy for others as they deal with whatever challenges they are facing, whether they be problems in marriage, addiction, rebellious teenagers, difficulty handling stress or conflict, insecurity, death, accident, injury...

But I have to get through my own personal crisis first, right?

George says I need to start saving a portion of everything I make. Okay, that makes a lot of sense, I should do that. I *will* do it. As soon as I'm doing a little better financially.

---

[1] Henry Wadsworth Longfellow

Dang! I just did it again.

I suffer from Special Case Syndrome — a mutation of destructive pride which quickly spreads throughout the mind. There are some serious side effects. Special Case Syndrome causes blindness and deafness. I can't see how I get in my own way. I don't hear what anyone else is saying. Their advice doesn't apply to me because I'm not like anyone else. *I'm special.*

I've seen this hundreds of times with my clients. I prescribe a solution for their anxiety or depression. They know it will help, and commit to do it as soon as they are feeling a little better. I just did the same thing. I will figure out, through my own staggering brilliance, how to do better and then I will apply the wise counsel of someone who has reason to know.

My friend, Brett Harward, teaches something about Special Case Syndrome that helps me realize how I am getting in my own way. In chapter ten of his book *The 5 Laws That Determine All of Life's Outcomes*, Brett relates this story:

> *Years ago I had the opportunity to attend a Special Olympics event in which my son, who has Down syndrome, was competing. One of the other participants was also a friend of mine, a tall, 16-year-old young man named David, and he was running the 50-yard dash. His mental handicap in life hadn't diminished his optimism or outlook. The race was run in heats and David was in the fourth heat.*
>
> *Since David wasn't especially motivated about winning, I stood with him near the starting line, attempting to get him excited and ready to "go for it" as his race approached. As his heat came up to the starting line, I asked, "So, are you going to win this race David?"*
>
> *He was in the first lane, and he proceeded to look down at the other participants in his heat. He then looked back at me and said with a big grin, "I can beat all these guys, they're all retarded."*

Brett is often criticized for using the word "retarded" in his story, but it was a direct quotation from a young man who saw everyone else around him as mentally challenged, except himself. *He* was special.

I'm doing the same thing. Special Case Syndrome has me thinking I am also ahead of the race when, in fact, I am way behind. I am a financial failure – failing, failed and flailing. My thinking is delayed, impeded, retarded, held back, lagging, hampered, fettered, encumbered, mired, hung up, myopic, arrested.

Remember the fellow who sat up all night wondering where the sun went?

It finally *dawned* on him.

And, as the early morning light spreads from the east, it dawns on me. Special Case Syndrome is the reason I'm not doing better. I better do something about it quick.

Is it time to listen to someone other than myself?

Coaches need coaching, counselors need counseling; and, yes, shrinks need shrinking. Until and unless I am willing to receive wise counsel from those who know things I don't, I will continue to struggle in my myopic misery.

We stop for gas in a small country town, Bliss, Idaho, population 275. This first stop is a welcome break from the psychological calisthenics I've been through all morning.

Bliss. How appropriate. Vicki and I have the best marriage I know of, and yet our bliss feels now somewhat like this dusty little town. Lots of heart but feeling run-down.

A shack across a weed-garnished lot near the gas station catches my attention. The ramshackle building bears a hand-painted representation of a pizza alongside the words, also hand painted, "Skinny Pig – Bliss's Best." It appears deserted. Dust covered remnants of someone else's dream.

Vicki and the kids head into the station for some morning refreshment while I refresh the minivan. As the kids stumble into the early light, I wonder if they realize our trip actually started four hours ago. They are just waking up — and, as it seems, so am I.

I turn toward the morning sun and jog in place as the old fashioned gasoline pump dial rattles off how much we won't have left to keep food on the table. I reach down to my toes then up to the sky for a good stretch. That makes me feel a little better.

As stiff legs and back loosen, I begin to loosen up inside. The cents spin past in a blur. I don't know why they even bother with pennies on gas pumps. The dollars click rapidly upward indicating the filling of the tank and the emptying of my debit account.

Is my life half full or half empty? It's an age-old question. I am determined to start my new prosperity perception by focusing on the filling of the tank, not the emptying of my bank account.

The pump handle releases with a loud clunk. The tank is full. As I avert my gaze from the painful financial truth staring back at me from the pump's numerical display, my eye catches a silvery glint at my feet. A shiny new dime.

I hang up the gasoline pump nozzle, my eyes fixed on the miniscule bit of surprise wealth at my feet. I reach down and retrieve the gift. It feels somehow symbolic. I slip it into my pocket with a feeling of gratitude. It's just a tenth of a dollar, but it feels like a seed to a bigger harvest. I must start somewhere, somehow. Why not here? Why not now? You've heard of stopping on a dime? Maybe I am starting on a dime!

Our journey to the beautiful state of Washington began over four hours ago. To my awakening family, it seems our journey started in Bliss Idaho. I guess it has.

I can see how Special Case Syndrome was getting in my way — I was getting in my own way. It isn't some uncontrollable metaphysical barrier to success and happiness, it is *choice*. My perspective feels fresh, like the smell in the air after the thunder and lightning have passed. The balance is restored.

Hey, why do I feel better? I haven't solved anything yet.

Chapter Two

The Problem Isn't Really the Problem
The Power of Discontent

Everything is okay in the end. If it's not okay, it's not the end.
~ Carolyn Myers

Necessity is the mother of invention. Difficult situations inspire ingenious solutions. During my early morning drive, I was stuck in the muck, frustrated, worried, dissatisfied. It was while in this state I finally saw how Special Case Syndrome was getting in my way, and also saw a possible solution. Happiness is a choice. This powerful realization came not in spite of, but *because* of the discontent I felt.

Discontent and unhappiness are not the same things. Necessity is, indeed, the mother of invention. Discontent is the father of creation. Difficult situations inspire ingenious solutions. Unhappiness may be one manifestation of discontent, but discontent is a more general concept. Sometimes discontent is uncomfortable or painful – and we feel unhappy. Some forms of discontent, like curiosity or anticipation, are pleasant – and we feel happy.

In whatever form or manifestation, discontent is essential to a healthy psyche. In fact, for the emotionally healthy, discontent is a natural precursor to happiness, joy, enthusiasm, vitality. For the emotionally unhealthy, discontent is assumed to be a precursor to disappointment and disaster.

Traditional thinking and conditioning puts a negative spin on discontent. One of the labels commonly assigned to something that creates discontent is "problem" – which bears its own stigma. We dislike discontent. We hate problems.

Or do we?

Perhaps we *think* we don't like problems because the vast majority of us have been conditioned from childhood to feel that having problems is bad and not having problems is good. Having a problem is generally seen as, well, a problem. Theodore Isaac Rubin, psychiatrist and author, disagrees. "The problem" he says, "is not that there are problems. The problem is expecting otherwise and thinking that having problems is a problem."

Captain Jack Sparrow, in *Pirates of the Caribbean* agrees, "The problem is not the problem. The problem is your attitude about the problem."

Having problems, therefore, is not really a problem. Believing that having problems is a problem – now, that's a problem!

Because of our conditioned belief that problems are bad, we tend to try to avoid them at all cost. Fact is, if we could avoid problems, there would, indeed, be a cost. Not having worrisome problems would cost us great solutions. It would also cost us the adventure of discontent, the thrill of creativity, and the joy of discovery. Great ideas, and inventions which bring us amusement, joy, better health, safety, contentment, a higher standard of living, would be lost if we didn't have problems to solve.

If discontent is the first step of creation and a precursor to pleasure, then we can feel a certain degree of pleasure immediately when a problem occurs. If, as soon as we feel discontent we recognize that something, small or great, is about to occur, be discovered, or invented, we immediately feel the pleasure of anticipation. Something better is on the way!

Discontent is the source or starting place of all inventions and advancements in science, from space shuttles to soup spoons, from the purchase of engagement rings to the acquisition of apologetic roses. Like lightning, discontent initiates the process of creation.

When our emotional environment or personal atmosphere is out of balance, there is a buildup of discontent usually showing up as discomfort, dissatisfaction, frustration, stress, disappointment, anxiety, pressure, sadness, pain, aggravation, a variety of other feelings we normally consider unpleasant – like a "negative charge" building up in our emotional atmosphere.

Then what happens?

Creativity strikes.

Creativity is the natural result of a perceived imbalance between what is and what could be. Not just what we desperately need, but also what we mildly desire. Both are discontent. Both are imbalance. Both are great.

When there is such an imbalance our human nature restores the balance with a small zap of creativity or a blinding flash of brilliance.

Discontent, including physical, mental, spiritual discomfort and pain, is simply a growing static charge on your skin that says, "Look out, here it comes" – a lightning bolt of creation to resolve the imbalance.

Tim Hansel, author of *You Gotta Keep Dancin'* said, "Pain is inevitable, but misery is optional." We have to feel pain, but we don't have to hate it.

What if we didn't feel pain? Wow! A life without pain – wouldn't that be great? Actually, no, it would not be great. In fact, without pain, life would be difficult in the extreme – possibly unlivable.

Occasionally a child is born with a rare condition called congenital analgesia. With otherwise normal neural functioning, these children either cannot feel, or are indifferent to, the sensation of pain. These children are a high risk for injuries in their mouth (from biting their own tongue) and eyes (because they can't tell there is a foreign object present) or other bodily injuries like burns, bruises, broken bones. Their inability to feel or respond to pain dramatically increases their risk of injury or susceptibility to disease.

Pain (discontent) serves us well. It is there for a reason. Just like pain tells us to remove our hand from a hot stove, discontent calls our attention to what is out of balance, missing, or otherwise needs our creative attention.

Scratching, for example, is inducing mild pain on purpose. We do it to relieve a physical problem or imbalance manifesting as an itch. We would not enjoy the scratch if we didn't have the itch. We would not enjoy the meal if we were not hungry. The drink would not satisfy if we did not thirst.

If we don't know something is wrong we are hardly in a position to make it right. Pain is a signal that something isn't right. That makes it just as valuable as the pleasure we seek from the relief of pain. The feeling of discontent – pain included – is our opportunity to enhance our lives. Discontent is a stimulus for creation. Pain is a guide to pleasure. Without discontent we'd still be living in a cave eating raw meat, picking our teeth with chipmunk ribs, without even a decent Saber-tooth tiger loincloth.

We are creators by nature. Many religions promote the idea that humans are more than just a creation; they are actual offspring of the Creator. As a child of the Supreme Creator, what would that make you? A creator. It's not that you can *become* a creator someday, you already are a creator. Just like a puppy is already a dog and a two year old child is already a person.

Watch a two-year-old eat (or wear) spaghetti. Some of it goes where it is intended and some is just a mess – or is it? Perhaps it *all* goes where the two year old intends it to go – some in his mouth and some in his hair and the rest – everywhere!

Is the child *wrong*? Is he sloppy, messy, undisciplined, incorrigible? No, he's creative. He was not content with the spaghetti being in the bowl. He wanted some of it in his mouth, some on his face, most of it on the walls and what's left decorating the top of his head.

Our creation trait begins when we are created, and persists throughout our lives. It isn't a virtue, it is simply a trait. It's a constant. We are constantly creating *something*. The question is, *what* are we creating? A masterpiece? A mess? Both? We create whatever our discontent drives or inspires us to create.

The fact is, we enjoy encountering problems (discontent) and if there are no obvious problems we generate a few (intentional discontent) so we can enjoy creating a solution (intentional creation). That's why we invent video games, board games, puzzles. We create discontent where it didn't exist before. We do it for the sheer enjoyment of creating a resolution. That's why we enjoy games and sports.

Why aren't there two footballs – two basketballs – two volleyballs – one for each team to play with so they don't have to fight over it? If we remove the conflict we remove the fun.

So if discontent is such a good thing, and we do it intentionally and naturally every day, what is the verb equivalent for "discontent" or "discontentment" which indicates our active role in the generation and experience of it?

Apparently the inventors of our English language have not acknowledged or even realized we value the process of discontent and creation. Or perhaps no intentional verb exists in English for discontent because it normally happens without intentional effort – naturally – like the flash of lightning on a stormy morning.

We can say we "feel discontent" or "experience discontent" or we can affirm that we "appreciate discontent." Perhaps we could invent a word for our intentional creation or enjoyment of discontent. How about, "discontenting."

What if we asked the designer of a golf ball, "Hey, what are you doing?"

"I'm just sitting here discontenting."

"What about?"

"I'm discontenting about how inconsistent in flight this smooth golf ball is. The old one flies better. I think it's because it's all nicked and dented. What if we nicked and dented the new one – while it's still new. Seems like a silly idea, but would it fly better? More consistently? Hmmm... Let's try it."

Of course we don't generally like misery and pain but we do enjoy curiosity and suspense. While curiosity seems more fun than pain, they are, nevertheless, the same thing – discontent – and they all tend to lead to the same thing – creation.

"Necessity is the mother of invention. Discontent is the father of creation." Every creation was invented to fulfill some need. Every invention was inspired by discontent. Discontent is here to stay. Good thing! Success and happiness depends on appreciating discontent, even creating it, not just wishing it would go away.

Some inventions are linked to obvious discontent. Anesthesia for surgery was invented because doctors felt discontent with their patients screaming. Did you think *patients* invented anesthesia? Other forms of discontent may be less dramatic or urgent, but still lead to creative and useful relief. Painting a landscape to hang on the wall where there is no window; or creating a different kind of hammer for a different kind of nail for a different kind of problem – like nailing into concrete instead of wood.

Discontent, is not, and never has been *negative*. Discontent is the impetus of learning, growth, progress. We don't feel discontent because life is bad, we feel discontent because things could be better. They could be bigger, smaller, faster, slower, stronger, softer, *more fun...* And when we are pathologically positive we actually appreciate and even enjoy discontent.

That seems so wrong! Do I seriously propose we could enjoy pain, problems, perplexity? Yes, I do. We enjoy life to its fullest when we enjoy *all* of life's adventure, including *and especially* the experience of solving problems. It fulfills one of our most basic human purposes.

We get bored. We find something to do. We open the paper to the crossword section or go out and buy a game to play. We roll the dice, make our move, pay the price for landing on the wrong square and enjoy dramatically groaning and complaining about it, or we enjoy the benefit of landing on a better square. We then hand the dice over to the other player, and wait with anticipation to see what happens next. We take the dice again and toss them to see what our next move will be. We now have again the opportunity to move closer to a win – or a loss – either way we feel discontent to just sit there occupying a space.

We want to play. We enjoy the potential of loss without which we could not enjoy the possibility of gain. In effect, we enjoy our discontent as much as our power of creation.

We see imbalance. We create balance. We see a problem. We create a solution. We find something which needs to be fixed. We fix it. When we don't see a problem, we create one. We look around, searching for something that isn't working or could be made better. We think about problems in disadvantaged countries or in the next county or in our back yard or on our desktop. Then we enjoy creating solutions for relief, fun, profit.

We accomplish the first important step in our process of becoming pathologically positive creators when we realize, perhaps for the first time in our lives, we actually need and appreciate the feeling of discontent. Our discontent positions us to enjoy creation.

In the process of answering the questions discontent raises and creating solutions to the challenges it brings, we enhance life for ourselves and others. We seek out problems. We solve them. We make a difference.

CHAPTER TWO

Chapter Three

The Feeling
Illuminating the Obvious

In all of living have much fun and laughter. Life is to be enjoyed,
not just endured.
~ Gordon B. Hinckley

As I work over chapter two, another summer thunderstorm serendipitously announces its arrival. I drop what I am doing and trot outside to watch. The dim light of evening is interspersed with bright, illuminating flashes of lightning. Adam, Lyndi, and I lie on the driveway in the rain to experience the contrast of warm pavement on our backs with cool droplets on our faces. I think I already mentioned that we are a little crazy about lightning storms.

We excitedly wait for the next burst of power as Mother Nature resolves the imbalance in the atmosphere. We don't wait long.

Suddenly, an exceptionally bright flash of cloud-to-ground lightning illuminates Vicki holding Mozzi, our ten month old Yorkie-Poodle mix. They find it entertaining to watch the crazier members of the family from the comfort of a dry porch. We already knew they were there. We could make them out in the dim light if we intentionally looked. The flash illuminates them.

Pathological Positivity lets us see things we already see, but didn't see clearly, or just didn't notice or pay attention to. *Pathological Positivity* illuminates the obvious.

Do you notice the feeling of your shirt?

You feel it all the time you are wearing it, but you don't notice the sensation unless you are reminded of it. If English is your primary language it probably did not occur to you that you are reading this book in English. Now that I bring it to your attention, you see it as an obvious fact. You didn't notice it, though, until I brought it to your attention — illuminating the obvious.

We seek meaning, peace, joy, success, pleasure, happiness. We all want to feel happy. That should be obvious. Pointing it out simply illuminates the obvious.

When we want something (discontent), we are noticing an imbalance which causes us to feel unhappy, displeased, or dissatisfied. Getting what we want resolves the imbalance and creates a sense of happiness, pleasure, satisfaction. Discontent fades away.

Then, just like a glorious lightning storm, the imbalance builds again to trigger more flashes of insight, creation of more brilliant solutions that bring greater satisfaction, joy, contentment.

The very word which describes the "negative" feeling of *dis*content implies the possibility of its "positive" opposite — feeling content. *Dis*satisfaction implies potential satisfaction. *Un*happy implies the possibility of happy. The positive word is embedded in the so called "negative" word. Within the problem lies the possibility of the solution.

We seek success and happiness. (There I go, illuminating the obvious again.) How can we tell when we are successful? When we feel successful, we feel good, right? We feel good about ourselves our achievements, our contributions. It is our universal, eternal quest to find the emotional state created by success — happiness, peace, joy, satisfaction, fulfillment, enlightenment, actuation, nirvana — a state wherein we look around ourselves and, *regardless of our circumstances* say, "This feels good."

What is this universally sought-after emotional state? We will simply call it *The Feeling*.

All we need is love.
Why?
To have *The Feeling.*

I want to get rich.
Why?
To get *The Feeling.*

Can I take your order?
I'll take a burger and curly fries.
Why?
For *The Feeling.*

What is your quest?
I seek the grail.
Why?
For *The Feeling.*

That is what we are after. *The Feeling. The Feeling* that life is good. *The Feeling* that life is great. This is our quest. We were born pre-programmed to desire and acquire *The Feeling.*

All theories, philosophies, policies, practices and tools are roads intended to lead us to that Rome — to feel good, better, great, to have *The Feeling.*

Success is accomplished through an accurate understanding and application of what brings us *The Feeling.*

Failure is accomplished through an erroneous understanding and application of what brings us *The Feeling.*

From a psychological perspective, having *The Feeling* is the most fundamental of all human needs. *Pathological Positivity* is the most efficient and effective method to acquire *The Feeling.*

Self-help and personal development sections of the bookstore are filled with *How to... The Three Steps to... Five Principles of... The Seven Irrefutable Laws of...*

What if some famous pieces were re-titled to reflect the fact that *The Feeling* is that which we seek? Unalienable rights set forth in the Declaration of Independence would become "life, liberty, and the pursuit of *The Feeling*." Viktor Frankl might have written *Man's search for The Feeling*. Stephen R. Covey's seminal work becomes *Seven Habits of Highly The-Feeling-ful People…*

Okay, I'm getting a little out of control; still, with all due respect to their brilliant authors, these influential writings are all designed to help us achieve the same goal — *The Feeling*.

"Sex, drugs, rock and roll." "If it feels good do it." The hedonistic mantra of the liberating (and in some ways, damaging) seventies was almost right (almost — that's why much of it was damaging). Perhaps it could have actually worked if they added; "if it still feels good when you sober up, do it;" or "if it will still feel good when your kids follow your example, do it."

Every decision we make is aimed at achieving *The Feeling*.

I propose this idea to a group of executives during a two day training. A seasoned CFO challenges that assertion. "I make my decisions based on reason, not emotion."

"Yes?" I respond, "Okay. How do you know when you have come to the right decision?"

"I study the data," comes the confident reply. "I crunch the numbers, analyze probable outcomes, and make my decision based on that."

"Good. How do you *know* when you have seen enough data and you have the right decision?"

"Because, well, it feels done. It…" He pauses. Grins. Sits down.

Yes, indeed. You are right. It is done because it feels done. It feels right. It feels finished. Therefore it is done, until you are again dissatisfied because it could be better — like denting an already perfect golf ball.

It is a self-evident, obvious, but previously unnoticed truth. We know we are done when we feel done, satisfied, convinced, resolved. We know we are right when it feels right. We *feel* good about our decision. We have *The Feeling*. When the golf ball's flight is stabilized, and we like it, we have achieved our goal.

Why purchase widgets rather than gadgets for the job?
Because they do the same thing and the widgets cost less.

Why do you care if you spend less?
Because my boss will be pleased with me.

Why do you want to please the boss?
Because the boss will let me keep my job.

Why keep your job?
Because I get a paycheck.

Why do you desire a paycheck?
So I can feed my family.

Why feed your family?
So they can survive and thrive.

Why do you want them to survive and thrive?
So I will have people around me that I love
– and they won't be dead.

Why have people around you that you love?
Because it feels good.

Ah, yes. There it is. *The Feeling*. We do everything we do in order to get *The Feeling*.

I have never actually interviewed an orangutan, elephant, or giraffe. I believe, however, that the entire animal kingdom shares this universal quest for *The Feeling* – on whatever level they operate. The main difference we seem to possess as humans is we can think about what we are thinking, and we can think about where we are headed. We can talk about it. We can write about it. We can notice it and become aware of this process that constantly operates in our psyche.

Discontent comes from noticing that *The Feeling* is missing or incomplete. Discontent triggers a process by which we create an invention, a philosophy, an idea, sometimes received in a flash of insight, which reestablishes the balance and achieves *The Feeling*.

The Feeling is available to us right now regardless of our circumstances. Pathologically positive people achieve *The Feeling* the moment we feel discontent – because we know discontent will lead us to more of *The Feeling*.

The Feeling is success.

Chapter Four

Metacognition
What Are You Thinking

Worry is the misuse of imagination.
~ Dan Zadra

Ask a ten-year-old in trouble, "*What* were you *thinking?*" It's generally not a question. It's a statement disguised as a question. It's actually an accusation. His response, "I don't know."

It's usually not an answer. It's a defense disguised as an answer. It's actually avoidance.

Ask the adult male sitting on the couch doing nothing, just staring into space, "What are you thinking?"

"Nothing," is the certain reply.

This time, it's true. He is, indeed, thinking about nothing – and he knows he is thinking about nothing.

Pastor Mark Gungor skillfully describes this phenomenon in his book, *Laugh Your Way to a Better Marriage.*

> *There's a special box in a man's head that most women don't know about. This particular box has nothing in it. We refer to it as the 'nothing box.' It's called that because it contains, well, nothing. It's just an empty box. And amazingly, of all the boxes stacked in a man's brain, his 'nothing box' is his favorite box. If given the opportunity, a man will always go straight to his 'nothing box.'*

He goes on to say, "Researchers have discovered that men do, in fact, have the ability to think about absolutely nothing and – get this – still breathe."

Women simply don't understand this.

When you draw a man's attention (commonly referred to as "nagging") to his sitting there thinking about nothing, you make him aware that he is thinking about nothing.

You thereby instigate metacognition — which is actually very cool.

Metacognition isn't thinking about what you are thinking, it is *noticing* you are thinking about what you are thinking. Yes, men, it might indeed be about nothing — your mate's protestations notwithstanding.

Do you ever catch yourself doing something silly and wonder, "What am I thinking?" You are initiating metacognition. What are *you* thinking, right now, as you read this? How and why are you thinking it? As you notice yourself thinking about your thinking process, you are fully engaged in metacognition.

It is amazing that we have the ability to think. Even more amazing is our ability to think about our thinking process — and be aware of it as it unfolds. Perhaps this is the main difference between us and the rest of the animal kingdom. Besides having a complex language and opposable thumbs, we can think about what we are thinking, and how and why we are thinking it.

Watching our mind process information, and our interpretations and reactions, puts us in a better position to choose. As we enhance our ability to choose, we enhance our power to live on purpose.

Viktor Frankl, author of *Man's Search for Meaning,* said, "Between stimulus and response there is a space. In that space is our power to choose our response. In our response lies our growth and our freedom."

Dr. Frankl is demonstrating metacognition. He helps his readers use their awareness of their own cognitive processes to make better choices. When we employ metacognition we can consider how we wish to respond, and thereby stay in control of our choices. Consequently, we live a more meaningful and purposeful life.

We live on purpose through better choices.

In the movie, *Groundhog Day*, Phil Connors (played by Bill Murray) gets stuck in a constantly repeating pattern of waking up to the same day every day. He gets a daily "do-over" whether he likes it or not. Every day he messes up in one way or another, then wakes the next morning on the same day and gets to try things differently.

Each day brings Phil a repeat of the same circumstances and challenges, but he remembers everything he learned and, after about a bazillion tries, he finally gets it right, wins the day, and the girl, and possibly lives happily ever after.

What if we could create a similarly useful (but less annoying) scenario for ourselves? We could limit our repeated scenario to three takes on every day. Day one is to see what is and consider how we would like to respond. Day two is to actually deal with it and think about the results. Day three is to do it over and get it right. Would that be great?

What helps us slow our reactions to difficult situations so we can observe, think and choose more appropriate responses? Metacognition.

Metacognition allows us to see the gap between stimulus and response. That gives us the opportunity to broaden the gap so we have time to think through our choices. How do we broaden the gap?

Just don't do anything – for a moment – especially when you are upset. Hang on. Hold on. Wait a minute. Push the pause button. Count to ten. Slow down. Breathe!

As we slow our reactions and broaden the gap between stimulus and response, we put ourselves in a position to choose how we interpret the situation and what we will do with it. Our reactions are then no longer reactions. They are intentional responses.

Those intentional responses guide our life.

In the last chapter you noticed the oft-unnoticed yet obvious feeling of your shirt on your back. You also became aware of the obvious, but not previously realized fact that you are reading this book in English. Then we noticed another previously unnoticed, but now obvious truth. That is, we all seek *The Feeling*. Metacognition – thinking about our thinking process – is another of those constant, obvious, but generally unnoticed phenomena. We not only notice these obvious truths, we now notice ourselves noticing them.

Metacognition –noticing our own thinking process – enhances our ability to question and consciously and conscientiously choose our interpretation of circumstances and events. We can then choose directions and behaviors that create circumstances likely to bring us *The Feeling* we seek.

Metacognition is a mental process which, like the GPS (Global Positioning System) in our vehicle, allows us to more clearly see where we are, where we are going, and how we are (or are not) getting where we wish to go. It helps us create the mental space where, even in the midst of turmoil, we can calmly decide if we like the direction of our thinking; then, if not, intentionally reset our mental compass, turn our thoughts around and let our pathologically positive minds guide us in a direction that makes more sense than the one which keeps us running into the same dead end.

As we think about our thinking, we gain a better position to direct our thinking. As we intentionally direct our thinking, we intentionally direct our life.

We live on purpose.

Chapter Five

Compared to what?
Coulda' Woulda' Shoulda' Works Both Ways

Giants are only giants compared to something smaller.
~ Paul H. Jenkins, Ph.D.

My youngest son, Brennan, recruits me to assist with his ninth grade biology bug-collecting assignment. He doesn't bother to ask Mom; he knows Vicki is not an aficionado of creepy-crawlies. He asks Dad. He came to the right place. I'm still a kid at heart. Insects are important – and fun. I know where some really big bugs live. We fire up the old Audi and head for Utah's west desert. Our mission: to find the fabled Mormon Cricket – the granddaddy of all crickets.

The west desert is normally infested with these monster crickets; however, after an exhausting search through hot sand, sizzling rocks and thorny, noxious desert weeds, we come to the sad conclusion that we must be too late in the season. We can't find a single cricket.

We dejectedly climb back into the Audi and turn back toward civilization. Then, just as we begin to pick up speed, we see something big and brown crawling across the road. Our search has met with success! I slam on the brakes. The dust cloud raised by our tires skidding to a stop obscures the air for a moment as we jump out with net and capture jar at the ready. We lunge for where we saw the creature.

In seconds, we skid to a stop ourselves, our hiking boots raising our own cloud of dust as our manly resolve teeters for a moment. Brennan gasps, "Wow! That is one humungous *spider!*"

We man up, push each other toward the beast, and after a few failed attempts which elicit shrieks (from my son, not from

27

me, of course), we finally capture the critter. We head for home, our trophy secured. It's a capture worthy of headlines.

Vicki, a self-diagnosed arachnophobic who has no interest in treatment for her condition, forbids us to bring the beast into the house. She refuses so vehemently that I feel sorry for the poor spider. He surely must sense her impolite refusal of simple hospitality.

The rest of the family also declines to witness our captive in the flesh. I, therefore, decide to photographically capture for posterity the result of our safari. Our quarry is indeed a specimen worthy of awe and reverence, as well as respect for the intrepid hunters who brought down into captivity this giant desert tarantula. Here is the first photo of him quarantined inside a box (Vicki is quite certain he is thinking "outside the box," hence her lack of hospitality). We are excited to post this for all to see and admire.

How disappointing. All this photo shows is a spider of indeterminate size. That's all. There is no comparison, no reference to show the size of this monster – or the box he's in. In fact, he appears to be rather small, maybe even cute; certainly not the fierce beast we conquered in the desert.

We realize our adoring and admiring fans will need a frame of reference in order to appreciate our bravery, so I toss a dollar bill in with our fuzzy friend. Now the picture makes comparative sense.

The spider is, of course, disappointed. He was expecting maybe a fifty or a hundred dollar bill.

Aragog (the giant spider from the *Harry Potter* series), as Brennan affectionately names the tarantula, is a seven legged fellow. I don't know his story, but he must have lost one of his legs in some fierce battle. I wanted to name him Peg Leg Pete, but my son thought that was lame.

How big is he? Compared to you or me, Aragog is a pipsqueak, weighing in at a mere ounce or two. But compared to other spiders, he is enormous!

Giants are only giants compared to something smaller.

Am I a tall man? I stand six foot two inches tall in my Vibram Five Finger shoes. Next to the NBA's top five shot blocking leader and fellow speaker, Mark Eaton, how do I look? There's a good reason his website is 7ft4 dot com. Next to Mark Eaton, I'm a pipsqueak, whether or not he is wearing any shoes at all.

Perception, comprehension, evaluation, require comparison. We generally compare what we see (or fear) to a mental image or standard with which we are already familiar. Our minds keep a record of things we have previously encountered, filed away under categories of large, small, desirable, undesirable, beautiful, ugly, etc. Such files are kept for the purpose of comparative choice so, for example, we can know when to run away!

What is this?
Looks like a spider.

Why?
He looks like a mental image of a spider stored in my experience database.
And this guy is huge!

Why do I think so?

Because the images in my experience database depict much smaller spiders.

That's why the dollar bill helps the picture. We have enough experience with spiders to know that most of them are quite small. "Quite small" means small in comparison to something else "quite big." Aragog looks cute in the first picture because he's just a fuzzy little spider. We have enough experience with dollar bills to know how big they are. Comparing Aragog to the bill puts things immediately into perspective, and we get it. He is, indeed, huge – by comparison.

Humans have a penchant for comparing in order to make sense of our perception of our experiences. We need this ability in order to effectively and efficiently observe a situation, evaluate it, determine if it's a good thing or not then decide what to do about it.

If we don't have directly applicable experience or immediately available comparative standards (like the dollar bill) against which to compare our current experience or view of a situation, we imagine or fabricate images or stories instead. These imagined images or stories are our most immediate standard for comparison.

I was surprised recently during a corporate team training where I showed the Aragog pictures. When the dollar bill was added, a man responds, "Oh, he's not as big as I thought."

He had imagined a much bigger spider. His thinking big probably serves him well in his sales profession!

Whether we imagine the spider to be bigger or smaller than it actually is, these imagined images are all we have until we are given something else against which to compare.

Consider the following experience:

You go to the office at your child's school to drop off a permission slip for a field trip. While you are at the front desk, a man in a ski mask barges in through the front door yelling incoherently and brandishing a pistol.

A police officer assigned to the school tackles the man from behind pinning the assailant's arms to his sides and bearing him to the floor. You hear the explosion of the gun going off at close range. You feel searing heat as the bullet rips through your shoe burning a painful groove along the outside of your foot.

The gunman is subdued, and taken to jail.

You get a quick trip to the emergency room.

Was this an unfortunate event or was it a fortunate one?
Was it unlucky or lucky?
Was it bad?
Was it good?

Your assessment of this situation, and your determination of whether it is good or bad, depends on comparison with an *imagined* alternate possible scenario.

Apply a touch of metacognition (think about your thinking) and watch your mind work as it creates your imagined alternate possible scenarios.

You can imagine an alternate scenario that is better than *what is*.

You can also imagine an alternate scenario which is worse than *what is*.

These imagined alternate scenarios provide a standard against which we evaluate our experience. Based on this evaluation, we decide if *what is* is better or worse than what else we might imagine.

Our feelings about the actual scenario will be governed by our feelings about our imagined alternate possible scenarios.

What is hangs suspended between better and worse until we decide which way to interpret it and how we will use that interpretation.

Intentionally choosing our imagined alternate scenario, therefore, serves two important purposes; evaluation of *what is,* and creation of *what is to be.* How we choose our imagined scenarios is an important psychological process behind *Pathological Positivity* and living on purpose a life you love regardless of immediate events or circumstances.

Purpose number one: Evaluation of *what is.*

Evaluation of *what is* drives our feelings about whether our immediate circumstances – and life in general – are good or bad. We can visualize something better which makes us feel worse, and we can imagine something worse which makes us feel better.

In the school shooting example, our alternate scenarios give us a basis for comparative analysis of *what is* which allows us to categorize it as being either fortunate because it coulda' been worse; or unfortunate because it woulda' been better (in fact, it shoulda' never happened).

Imagined better possible scenario: I coulda' been somewhere else this morning. The bullet woulda' missed me. That cop shoulda' taken him down faster. I'm really unlucky!

Imagined worse possible scenario: Wow! That guy coulda' killed *everyone* in the room. I woulda' been killed! It was mid-morning. That cop shoulda' been on his break. I'm really lucky!

"Coulda' woulda' shoulda'" works both ways.

Our life, then, is not determined by our mood, as much as it is determined by our *mode!*

In *noxious negativity* mode we imagine better alternate scenarios than the one we are experiencing. Because these alternate scenarios look better than what actually happened, *what is* looks pretty bad by comparison. We evaluate the shooting incident based on comparison with an imagined scenario in which there was no gunman and no shot was fired, because a clairvoyant police officer subdued the guy right after he got out of bed and before he could cause any kind of trouble at all (Tom Cruise in *Minority Report*). Thus what actually happened seems bad by comparison.

This so-called *positive scenario* of what coulda' woulda' shoulda' happened – but didn't – promotes a noxiously *negative* behavior – whining.

Contrast this with *Pathological Positivity* mode, in which we imagine alternate scenarios which are worse than what we are experiencing. For example, we imagine the tragic events of Columbine or Sandy Hook, creating a much *worse* alternate scenario than being shot in the foot. Because these alternate scenarios look much worse than what actually happened, *what is* looks good by comparison. This so-called *negative* rendition of what coulda' woulda' shoulda' happened creates a *positive* reaction.

We experience relief, even gratitude, about what took place. How marvelous that this particular gunman was subdued by a police officer who just happened to be in the right place at the right time. How fortunate that I was shot in the foot, rather than between the eyes. How lucky and blessed we are that the children were unharmed.

This promotes a pathologically positive behavior – grinning through the pain.

Jill Stevens embodies the concept of constructive evaluation of what is – even in a battle zone. She is the author of *It's All Good*. Nicknamed Utah's GI Jill, she joined the National Guard just six months before 9/11, then served an eighteen month tour of duty in Afghanistan.

Jill declares that positive evaluation is essential to the mental health of our war fighters. She made a pathologically positive choice about how to personally and emotionally deal with all of the "bad" things she encountered in war. Her positive approach to tough circumstances was infectious. She encouraged her fellow soldiers to adopt a similar position toward their circumstances.

This battle hardened, yet heart softening, soldier was voted Miss Utah in 2007, and "America's Choice" attendant in the 2008 Miss America pageant. (When she was honored at the pageant, she dropped to the floor of the stage and began doing push-ups.)

Jill is right. *It's All Good* – especially by comparison.

Through the intentional application of a pathologically positive interpretation that what we have is much better than it might have been, we immediately achieve *The Feeling* – even in a situation that most would consider bad.

Pathologically positive people are not faking *The Feeling*. We actually see *what is* as good – because it is. We therefore live in *The Feeling* as we establish the comparative positive value of our experiences against what could have happened and feel appreciation, even gratitude, for our circumstances – even if others might see it as negative.

This is where some caution is warranted. Our conditioned positive reaction to painful events can be irritating to others. Being relatively happy and relaxed when others think we should be upset and anxious can cause others to feel that pain is being ignored, minimized, not validated – especially if the pain is theirs. Therefore, while keeping a positive perspective yourself, be sure to approach other's feelings with care, caution, empathy and compassion, remembering that *Pathological Positivity* is primarily intended for personal use. When applied too quickly *to someone else* it may trigger a negative reaction because they think we just don't get it.

But we do "get it." We get *The Feeling*.

We could be sitting on the ground with our world crashing down around us with a grin on our faces experiencing *The Feeling*.

Does this sound a little crazy? Crazy or not, you have *The Feeling*. That is our quest. The reason for living. To get *The Feeling*, especially during tough times, and help others do the same.

PRODUCT WARNING

Pathological Positivity is intended primarily for personal use. Use extreme caution when attempting to apply to others. Moderate to severe irritation may occur in case of in-your-face-contact.

If this happens, flush generously with empathy and maintain positive pressure while increasing the dosage of compassion.

Pathological Positivity has now achieved purpose number one – a positive evaluation of what is. We are successful because we have *The Feeling*. We are pathologically positive people who habitually make the best of every situation. We use our imagined worse possible scenarios to make *what is* look good. We feel good because we see *what is* as good.

We are happy – here – today – right now. This is the beginning of living life on purpose driven by *Pathological Positivity*.

Purpose number two: Creation of *what is to be.*

Now that we are aware of our evaluation process and can grace it with *Pathological Positivity*, we are in position to create a better *what is to be*.

We have used our imagined alternate scenarios to evaluate *what is* as good in comparison with what could have been. Now we move into creation mode and use our imagined alternate scenarios to envision something better than *what is*.

This creates positive energy and direction for our power to create a better *what is to be.*

As we experience discontent with *what is* and imagine a better possible scenario of what could be, we intentionally guide our creative effort to bring into existence something better than *what is.*

In the story of *The Spyglass,* Richard Paul Evans spins a tale about a traveler who visits a poor kingdom that is run down and weary. The traveler presents the king with a magic spyglass which allows the king and his subjects to look at any part of the kingdom and, instead of the relatively dismal *what is,* they would see a beautiful scene of *what could be.*

Houses in disrepair appear to be beautiful cottages. Dried up yards appear to be lush gardens. Haggard downtrodden peasants look energetic and happy.

These magically imaged better possible scenarios become blueprints for the future. As the king and everyone else in the kingdom see something better, they begin to work toward that image. They dramatically improve their circumstances and build the wonderful kingdom they see through the magic spyglass.

In a speech entitled *Envision Utah,* Salt Lake City Mayor, Ralph Becker, then Minority Leader of the House of Representatives, presented a similarly inspiring idea. He said:

> *It was the Second week of August, 1847. Our Founding Fathers stood upon Ensign Peak and looked out over the Salt Lake valley. They saw beautiful cities and towns with wide streets, civic centers and green shaded commons. They saw sturdy, well designed homes with front porches and backyard swings. They saw police and fire protection and clean running water...*
>
> *They were looking at sand and sagebrush. But they saw beautiful homes, well laid out cities and towns, and well planned communities.*

He then laid out a new plan for enhancing his already beautiful state.

I sometimes give my clients a special (meaning "strange") assignment. Go out into the community, and do something to make things worse. I tell them they have thirty minutes in which to accomplish this.

They stare at me like I'm completely off my rocker. It's a silly suggestion. Why would they want to do something to make things worse?

Then we have a discussion about how quickly their mind can imagine half a dozen ways to make things worse. They wouldn't have to go "out into the community" to accomplish it. And it wouldn't take thirty minutes.

The assignment is admittedly silly, but illuminates the obvious. It is as obvious as a menu with only two options. Imagine the waiter handing you a menu and saying, "From our menu, you may select something worse, or something better than what you already have. Those are the only two items today. Are you ready to order, or do you need more time to decide?"

Our ability to imagine worse scenarios is not for the process of creation because we are working towards something better, not worse, than the current *what is*.

Pathologically positive people only use imagined worse scenarios for evaluation – to see in context, and feel better about difficult current or past situations.

They focus on an imagined better scenario, a *positive* possibility, to create a better future.

Creating a life we love and living it on purpose requires that we do something outside the ordinary. Ordinarily, ordinary people do not do anything out of the ordinary, that's why their lives are ordinary. Extraordinary people do extraordinary things – like appreciating *what is*, no matter what *what is* is. That's why their lives are extraordinary.

When we do something extraordinary, what do people say? "That's crazy!" Yes, hence the term, *pathological.* Remember, though, pathologically positive people are *called* pathological because they *seem* crazy, not because they *are* crazy.

Sometimes we resist *Pathological Positivity* because, while it may not seem out-and-out crazy, it feels like we are not being realistic.

What is real?

What is, is real.

What we interpret, reinterpret, create or recreate on purpose with *Pathological Positivity* becomes *what is* – and thereby becomes real.

We feel successful as soon as we appreciate *what is* as good, and see *what is to be* as even better. Like a child excited to open birthday presents, the pathologically positive relish and enjoy the anticipation of great things to come – no matter how things seem here and now.

We get *The Feeling* even before what is coming arrives!

Success, therefore, doesn't *bring* happiness – happiness *is* success. By putting ourselves into this constructive frame of mind where we have *The Feeling* now and excitedly anticipate more of *The Feeling* later, we become successful – immediately.

Our alternate scenarios are imaginary, made up, fabricated, for comparison or for creation. None of the imagined alternate scenarios are *what is* – yet. Since they are all fabricated, we can choose which serves us best for evaluation and then for creation. We focus on that, create it, and enjoy it.

We thereby live on purpose with *Pathological Positivity*, continually and naturally creating the life we love, by evaluating *what is* in the light of what could be worse, and *what is to be* in the light of what could be better.

Chapter Six

Power Tools
Plug This In and Give Er' a Whirl

A hammer neither builds nor destroys; it simply yields to the will
of the wielder.
~Paul H. Jenkins, Ph.D.

Because we can always imagine our situation to be better, there is always another project to do on the weekends. One such weekend project brings me to my knees. I'm kneeling on the hard cold cement of our basement bathroom shower, discontenting over the location of the shower drain and puzzling over the problem of moving said drain six inches to the south – in a six inch thick concrete floor. This is no small task for a guy who considers "work" to generally involve wearing a dress shirt, slacks, and shiny shoes.

My next door neighbor, Mike, is a professional builder. He is brought in for a consultation. He has seen this kind of challenge dozens of times before. He sees what needs to happen and helps me see it too. We will figure out which direction the drain pipe runs, break up the concrete in that area, dig down to the pipe, cut off the old pipe, add a fitting of some kind, reconnect the pipe, and fill up the hole again. Simple.

A week later, I'm still on my knees whacking away at the concrete with hand-held chisel and two pound sledge hammer.

"Simple" and "easy" are not the same thing.

My other neighbor Darren, proprietor of Darren's Handyman Service, pops in to see how things are coming with my project. He watches bemused then amused; chuckles and leaves, reassuring me that he will be right back.

A few moments later I wipe the burning sweat from my eyes and look up to see Darren hefting something that looks like a weapon of mass destruction. "Here, plug this in and give er' a whirl."

It's a hammer-drill, little brother of the jackhammer. It has a chisel on one end like the one I am using, only about twice as big; a heavy middle section with handles and a trigger; a thick electrical power cord extending from the other end. This power tool connects with high voltage lightning power. Awesome! No comparison to my puny little hammer and chisel.

Power tools are designed to make our work faster, easier, and more efficient. They tend to be most effective when we plug into a power source, find the "on" switch, and engage the system. In fact, with no positive power source, that heavy hammer-drill is awkward and even less effective than my primitive hand-chiseling technique.

I'm not talking here about getting better and better at using a hammer and chisel, although that will certainly occur as I use it. I'm talking about moving to an entirely new level with a tool that is many times more powerful than what I am used to.

I'm talking about moving up to a level of thinking which is infinitely more effective in building the life we love.

Not just thinking better at the level we are used to thinking; but thinking better at a level we have never before even thought about thinking.

As we discussed in chapter five, no matter how bad things are, we can always imagine something worse than our current situation – or we can imagine something much better.

The process of *Pathological Positivity* is simple and specific to each of our two purposes, evaluation and creation. Our mind is a power tool for building a better life. We already use it naturally and instinctively for good or ill. We can also learn to use it on purpose, conscientiously, for good.

Another important thing to know about power tools is that they are, well, powerful. They can be as dangerously destructive as they can be positively productive – depending on how they are used. It is extremely important, therefore, to follow the guidelines and instructions for safe and proper use.

It is the same with our mind. It is a magnificent power tool that can make magic and miracles or mess and mayhem.

Power tools have owners' manuals and safety guidelines for their proper use. Like any power tool, misuse of our greatest power tool – our mind – can cause detrimental destruction. Conversely, proper use of this amazing power tool creates positive perception, powerful imagined scenarios, and productive plans that lead to solutions for even the most difficult problems.

As is true with most natural skills, talents and strengths, our ability to imagine and interpret using this power tool called mind, can be controlled, strengthened, trained, refined. This requires some serious commitment.

Becoming truly pathologically positive is not for the faint of heart.

In his book, *The Genius in All of Us*, David Shenk references something which is now quite commonly known. Rather than being the result of genetics or inherent genius, truly outstanding skill in any domain is rarely achieved with less than ten thousand hours of practice over ten years' time.

David suggests that this type of practice "requires a constant self-critique, *a pathological restlessness*, a passion to aim consistently just beyond one's capability so that daily disappointment and failure *is actually desired*, and a never-ending resolve to dust oneself off and try again and again and again" (emphasis added).

As the ideas in this book resonate with you, you will naturally feel a desire to improve your own ability to apply positivity in every aspect of life. The sooner you take action and begin to practice, the sooner you will experience powerful results. The *Pathological Positivity* Prescription at the end of this book provides a structure by which anyone can begin immediately to practice *Pathological Positivity*. The prescription puts a new tool into our hands (or mind in this case). It is not an exercise to get better at our old way of thinking, but an exercise to get us to a new kind of thinking – a new level of cognition and processing.

Our ability to imagine alternate scenarios is an incredibly important and useful power tool in remodeling our lives and living with greater purpose. Living on purpose is the plan – the blueprint. *Pathological Positivity* is the guide to safe, constructive, and productive operation of our God-given mental power tool in building the life we love. Not just the life we *will* love, the life we love the instant we begin the creation process. In other words, *right now*.

No longer the inefficient hammer and chisel that just taps away at a tough situation, the mind becomes a hammer-drill that tears away old stuff, and makes way for a new possibility – the life you love.

The science and logic behind *Pathological Positivity* first engages metacognition to see, and then choose how to properly apply our imagination to evaluate our current situation and guide our creation of what is to be. Metacognition, as you recall, allows us to notice we are doing this. Noticing we do this creates the opportunity to choose how we will use our mental power tool in creating the highest likelihood of achieving or enhancing *The Feeling*.

Noxious negativity uses the exact same power tool for destructive purposes.

Can you imagine what a hammer drill would do to a grand piano? It would become a tangle of piano wire, splinters of shiny black wood and shattered ivory keys in a sad, dusty, pile. Our mind can be even more destructive. Misuse of this amazing power tool makes messy piles of our emotions. Negative judgment of ourselves and our lives mixed with ominous foreboding of a dark future is the classic recipe for depression and despair – the beginning of the end of what we coulda' shoulda' enjoyed if we just woulda'.

Cue up the theme song of a couple of sad ol' fellers on the classic television down home variety show, *Hee Haw*:

> Gloom, despair, and agony on me
> Deep dark depression, excessive misery
> If it weren't for bad luck,
> I'd have no luck at all…

Evaluating *what is* as bad, and anticipating *what is to be* as even worse, creates anxiety and depression – "gloom, despair, and agony" – psychopathy.

Pathological Positivity engages our imaginative mental power tool in a constructive way, preventing psychopathy and promoting prosperity. Imagined scenarios which look worse than *what is* serve as compelling evidence that *what is* is good. Imagined scenarios which look better than *what is* guide our creation of *what is to be*. As we intentionally enhance our ability to do this, and follow the safety guidelines of *Pathological Positivity*, we plug in our mental power tool and *immediately* create the life we love.

CHAPTER SIX

Chapter Seven

Posiception
The Power of Positive Perception

[It's] the lens through which your brain views the world that shapes your reality. And if we can change the lens, not only can we change your happiness, we can change every single educational and business outcome at the same time.
~ Shawn Achor

In her brilliant presentation *On Being Wrong*, Kathryn Schulz said, "The miracle of your mind isn't that you can see the world as it is, it's that you can see the world as it isn't."
We are, indeed, quite capable of clearly seeing an alternate reality. We do it all the time. In chapter four, we discussed metacognition; in chapter five, our ability to see an alternate reality; in chapter six, the power tools needed to build it.

How does the world appear when you put on glasses with green tinted lenses? You are in the Emerald City. Your lawn looks much better. Your family, not so much.

Are you really in the Emerald City? No, it just appears to you that you are.

Our perception does not alter *the* world – it alters *our* world. Just because the world looks green, doesn't mean it *is* green.

What we look at is *not* darkened, colored, altered, changed when we put on tinted glasses. The world remains constant. *How we see it* changes.

In the same way, our perception seems to color things but, in fact, does not alter reality. Our perception affects how we personally experience and deal with reality, which may empower us to alter circumstances from this point forward, but perception alone does not alter what is.

While neither negative nor positive perceptions change the world, our perception does change *us*. *We* then change the world.

Dr. George Stratton was a psychologist studying perceptual adaptation, the ability of the brain to perceive as "normal" something that has actually been purposefully altered.

In 1896, Dr. Stratton conducted research involving spectacles which altered the wearer's perception so everything appeared to be upside down. Dr. Stratton wanted to see what would happen if someone were to wear the specialized lenses for an extended period. He postulated that we would adapt, but was not certain how; hence, the experiment.

He couldn't get anyone to sign up for this upside-down study, so he put the glasses on himself.

Can you picture George trying to get around, as he bumps into things and stumbles through his own house wearing these lenses that turned his world upside-down? Imagine the difficulty of performing even basic tasks like filling up (or filling down) a glass of water at the sink, then trying to drink it.

After a few days George got used to the view through the upside-down glasses. A few days of practice made it so he wasn't bumping into things as much or spilling things as often.

On the eighth day, something amazing happened. He woke up one morning and the world no longer looked upside-down. George's mind had reinterpreted his upside-down world, corrected the image, and somehow made everything look right side up – and he was still wearing the glasses.

However positive or negative we may be, we grow accustomed to our perception and it becomes *our* reality, regardless of how altered from *actual* reality our perception may be.

How miraculous it is, that our mind can so adjust and adapt our perception and perspective. Dr. Stratton and other researchers after him have repeatedly shown that the human mind can adapt itself to perceive as "normal" something which is not.

Is that good news? It depends on whether your perception is habitually constructive or habitually destructive.

Our perception of reality is altered and alterable by the powerful tool called "mind." Indeed, it is truly "mind over matter."

It is commonly said, "We don't see things as *they* are; we see things as *we* are." From subtle to severe, what we see is generally filtered through colored lenses – lenses that have been tainted, altered, colored by our experience.

Perception is how we see. How we frame what we see is paradigm. Perception, right or wrong, clear or colored, creates our paradigm.

In Joel Arthur Barker's book, *Paradigms,* he describes the evolution of the definition of "paradigm." The original English definition comes from the Greek *paradeigma* meaning example, pattern, or model. The scientific community adopted and expanded the concept of paradigm to include traditions *or shared assumptions* in a particular area of study or research.

Thomas Kuhn, a scientific historian and author, suggested that scientists who share a paradigm are committed to the same standards and rules of scientific practice.

Shared paradigms can be true or untrue, accurate or inaccurate, constructive or destructive, hopeful or despairing.

Moving beyond the adapted scientific definition of paradigm, other authors cited by Barker refer to paradigm as a framework for understanding and comprehending the world. In *Powers of the Mind,* Adam Smith suggests that paradigm is the way we see the world.

As fish view water, in which they swim, so we view reality. A fish lives the span of his life in the midst of his watery world. It is difficult for him to imagine any other reality. Why would he, anyway? The fish's perception of the world works just fine –

for the fish. What the fish is missing is the realization of a parallel universe where fishermen lie in wait to snare him.

In *An Incomplete Guide to the Future*, Willis Harmon defines paradigm as our "basic way of perceiving, thinking, valuing, and doing associated with [our] particular vision of reality." What he says next is particularly important. "A dominant paradigm is seldom if ever stated explicitly; it exists as unquestioned, tacit understanding which is transmitted through culture and to succeeding generations through direct experience rather than being taught."

In chapter three, I called your attention to the obvious but previously unnoticed fact that you are reading this book in English. Had I written this book in Finnish (jos olisin kirjoittanut tämän kirjan Suomeksi) you would definitely notice that – unless Finnish is your default language paradigm.

In high school, I made friends with Tomi – an exchange student from Finland. His heavy Finnish accent set him apart from all of the other kids. We teased him a little, partly because of his accent, partly because in those days we didn't know the meaning of "politically correct," and partly because of his good-natured willingness to join in the banter.

A few years later, I am living in Helsinki, struggling with my rudimentary understanding of Finnish. The tables now are turned.

Tomi is back in Helsinki studying at the university. I look him up. As we visit with each other, now speaking *his* native language, I am astounded by his level of intellect and sophistication. I always assumed he was bright but, until I experienced him in a different paradigm, I never realized he was brilliant.

English, Finnish, Swahili; *something* occupies our primary language paradigm. Whatever cultural language we are used to isn't the only right language – but it seems so when we have been trained, taught, educated, conditioned to see, interpret, and describe our world in that language. For most of us, it is difficult to learn to think and interpret in a language other than the one we are used to.

Being immersed in our own paradigm often leads to problematic interactions with others who operate with a completely different paradigm.

A scene from the hit television series, *Cheers,* shows Carla and Rebecca conversing at the bar; with Sam and Norm chiming in. Rebecca is admiring a beautiful bouquet of roses Carla received from her boyfriend, Eddie.

Rebecca: Oh Carla, those are gorgeous. Who sent them?

Carla: Who do you think?

Rebecca: Oh isn't Eddie sweet? Oh, why can't more men send flowers?

Sam: I didn't know Mormons couldn't send flowers.

Rebecca: I said *more men,* not Mor-*mons.*

Sam: I know they can't dance.

Norm: No Sammy, that's the Amish.

Sam: Why can't Mormons send flowers?

Rebecca: They *can.*

Sam: Then what are you talking about?

Rebecca: I just wish someone would send me some roses!

Sam: Why does it have to be a Mormon?

Rebecca: [storming out of the room, exasperated] Oh!

Sam: [muttering to himself] With some people, you just can't discuss religion.

Rebecca and Sam clearly have different paradigms. The conflict between them is funny to us because we see both paradigms. Rebecca thinks Sam is a moron (not a Mormon). Sam, on the other hand, thinks Rebecca is unreasonable and histrionic.

Sam's reactions are based on an inaccurate perception. He is unaware that he and Rebecca see through different lenses; have different paradigms; speak a different language.

Great for the television audience. Not so great for their relationship.

Again, "A dominant paradigm...exists as unquestioned, tacit understanding arrived at through direct experience rather than being taught."

It is normal to be unaware of another's paradigm. It is also normal to be unaware of your own paradigm.

I said "normal." I didn't say "effective."

Our brain tends to default to whatever program is already installed and running, especially when we are under pressure. As our mental computer's operating system, paradigm runs unnoticed in the background, while affecting our perception, interpretation, reaction and response to the world around us — and everyone in it. We tend not to question our programmed paradigms unless we have a reason to do so (like my calling your attention to the fact that you are reading and understanding this in a particular language).

Changing a paradigm can be as difficult as learning a new language — but it is worth the effort. Our programmed paradigms define and determine our experiences, our relationships, ourselves — everything.

Not only do we generally accept without question our current paradigm, we also tend to see evidence which supports what we already believe, while not noticing contradicting information or interpreting it in a way that supports what we already believe. We tend to accept or selectively filter out evidence in a way that supports our current set of beliefs. In the industry, we call this tendency "confirmation bias."

Are flowers from hubby evidence that he is trying to hide something? Twelve red roses become twelve *read* roses. Something is being read into the roses. Failure to question our assumptions or suspicions gets us into trouble in business and at home. Roses can be read as an expression of love just as easily as a cover for guilt.

Paradigms evolve naturally from experience. We don't normally cultivate paradigms scientifically or intentionally. We are, however, entirely capable of cultivating them on purpose. We can defeat negative or destructive confirmation bias and cultivate positive, constructive confirmation bias instead.

Our minds are like fertile earth, ready and willing to produce an abundance of whatever is planted. The ground doesn't care. My little vegetable garden thrives under my care. There is a weed patch in a neglected spot nearby. Those weeds also thrive.

Weeds are the default flora and are naturally inclined to sprout and grow without interference. In fact, over the centuries, the soil has become so thoroughly impregnated with their seed, that weeds will quickly take over if one's garden is left untended. Likewise, left unattended, we soon find the garden of our mind overgrown with the noxious weeds of negativity, fear, doubt.

When we intentionally plant and cultivate productive positive paradigms, they also grow and thrive as long as we conscientiously care for our garden, pulling the weeds as they sprout.

Is it possible to see the world as it actually is? Are we really capable of viewing the world directly and not through tinted lenses? Can we cultivate a mind filled with healthy, *accurate,* positive paradigms – and weed out the noxious negativity thorns and thistles? Yes we can. When we do we are in better position to perceive our world as it really is, and cultivate what will be to be what we would like it to be.

CHAPTER SEVEN

52

Chapter Eight

The Choice
Victim or Agent

*He is a wise man who does not grieve for the things which he has
not, but rejoices for those which he has.*
~ Epictetus

How would we respond to the world *if we could see it
clearly?*

In this book so far we have begun to identify two
primary views of our world – two determinant paradigms –
noxious negativity and *Pathological Positivity*.

Each of these paradigms tends to manifest in a certain
mode. When we operate in the *Pathological Positivity* paradigm, we
typically respond in what we call "agent mode." When we
operate in the noxious negativity paradigm we typically respond
in "victim mode."

A "mode" is a designated condition or status for
performing a task or responding to a problem. Victim mode is
formed from a belief that we are *victims* of circumstance. Agent
mode is formed from a belief that we are *creators* of
circumstance – by manipulation or interpretation.

While dealing with life's little surprises, we normally shift
back and forth between *Pathological Positivity* and noxious
negativity. We also switch modes from victim to agent,
operating under whichever mode seems to work for us, or
whatever mode we have been conditioned to operate in, under
the circumstances, especially considering the paradigm we are
in.

Until we achieve perfection, nirvana, divine enlightenment,
we are never permanently in either paradigm or mode. This

switching about is not a flawed human characteristic. It is normal.

This chapter is, therefore, about different approaches to problems – positive or negative perceptions, paradigms and modes – it is not about positive or negative *people*.

The noxious negativity paradigm promotes a victim mode of response.

In this discussion, "victim" does not refer to a victim of crime, abuse, or accident. "Victim" is a mode for performing a task or responding to a problem. It is a mode that produces an unproductive reaction to a world seen through the tinted and tainted lenses of noxious negativity. "He's just being a victim." "She's really playing the victim."

"Being a victim," then, is not what we *are*. It is what we *are doing*. It is how we react to our circumstances, in the moment. Being a victim really means we are operating in a victim mode. Our perception of our world (seen through tainted noxious negativity lenses) is dark and dangerous. Our victim mode seems perfectly appropriate, based on our perception of reality in the moment.

Victim mode is much more than self-perception, it is *everything* perception. When we are in the noxious negativity paradigm, we not only see *ourselves* as victims, we *see as victims*. We experience, react, and respond to problems, and even to our own creative discontent, as victims.

In this mode, we feel very little sense of control or choice – things just happen to us – we feel a sense of powerlessness – and we suffer.

This is not a judgment. It is merely a professional observation, a method of coding behavior. Remember, victim mode is something *everyone* does from time to time – including me – because we are human. Instead of telling each other and ourselves to "stop being a victim" perhaps a more helpful line of thought would be to notice when and how we slip into victim mode, and assess whether that's working for us and those around us — especially those who depend on us for leadership.

If it isn't, then we might try the agent mode and see if that serves us better.

The *Pathological Positivity* paradigm promotes an agent mode of response.

In this discussion, an agent is one who acts or has the power to act.

Like "victim," "agent" is also a mode for performing a task or responding to a problem. It refers to the mode we are in when we see things as they really are, appreciate what we see, and accept our responsibility to deal with that reality constructively and positively.

It is a productive reaction to a world seen with the clear insight of *Pathological Positivity*.

As agents, we see and interact with our world in a very different way than we do when we are in victim mode. As agents we see opportunities, not problems. Actually, we do see problems; but we interpret them as opportunities.

We take the position that everything happens for a reason — or we make a positive reason for everything that happens and move forward accordingly.

Like victim mode, agent mode is much more than self-perception, it is *everything* perception. In the *Pathological Positivity* paradigm we not only see *ourselves* as agents, we *see as agents*. It is what we *do*. It is how we react to our circumstances. We experience, react, and respond to problems, and to our own creative discontent, as agents.

Agents see life as it is, not as it isn't. We see bright possibilities, not dark impossibilities. We choose to act, rather than be acted upon. In this mode, we feel a sense of control or choice no matter what happens.

Victim mode creates a need for blame.

While in victim mode we tend to assign guilt, fault and blame, rather than focus on taking responsibility.

Everything that goes wrong is seen, through noxious negativity lenses, as being someone's fault – usually someone else! Something or someone else is the source of our problem or pain; likewise, something or someone else is the solution. The government, Mom, Dad, God, the devil, our first grade teacher, the guy who stole our wallet, the abuser in our dark past – they caused the problem, therefore, they have to fix it. If they won't, or aren't around to fix it, we're stuck. We are victims. We are stuck until someone else un-sticks us.

I used to do child custody evaluations for the court. It was my job to analyze and deal with some of the nastiest family fights you could imagine. Guess who these frustrated couples – now angry individuals – blame for the misery in their life. Right. Each other.

How soon do they expect their ex will make everything okay for them? After all, the ex has, in the victim's mind, caused the problem in the first place. Since their ex broke it, they expect the ex to fix it.

They have quite a long wait ahead of them.

When not busy blaming their ex, noxiously negative victims blame me, the judge, the attorney, the system, even the institution of marriage and the churches who sponsor such. Blame is the hallmark of victimhood. It is compelling evidence that they have noxious negativity glasses perma-pasted on their face.

Blame is blame, no matter whom or what we blame. Blaming others is blame. Blaming ourselves is still blame. When we blame ourselves, we are still *seeing as* a victim. If we blame some*thing* else, we are a victim of circumstances. If we blame some*one* else, we are the victim of their behavior. If we blame *ourselves* we are the victim of our own flawed judgment.

Noxious negativity persists to insist that someone else brought us to this point. It's their fault. Or, if we can't find someone else to blame, we have to sigh and fault ourselves. It's our fault. That's how noxious negativity works – and it *doesn't* work.

What causes the victim mentality is blame. What perpetuates blame is the victim mentality. It's a self-perpetuating downward spiral into the black hole of noxious negativity. How soon will the economy, the government, the abuser, the ex, the weather, or the devil fix what is broken? Never.

Agent mode creates a sense of responsibility.

The pathologically positive accept responsibility. Guilt, fault, and blame are irrelevant in agent mode.

Daniel Webster's on-line dictionary says "responsibility" is synonymous with "blame, fault, liability." "It's my responsibility" is, therefore, commonly taken to mean, "It's my fault."

Mr. Webster, isn't quite accurate, however; at least not from a *Pathological Positivity* perspective. In agent mode, "responsibility" has absolutely nothing to do with "fault." Responsibility is, in fact, the polar opposite of blame. To accept responsibility simply, and quite literally, means to accept or acknowledge our ability to respond to a situation without regard to whom or what caused it. We accept our response ability.

Perhaps, then, we should spell the word "response-ability." Or, better yet, "respons*ability*." We'll spell it this way from now on in this book. Other authors and speakers spell it this way too, so there is precedence.

I am driving down the freeway (actually, pathologically positive people drive *up* the freeway), absorbed in a pathologically positive podcast, and I blow right past my turnoff – the last exit before the next state. I realize my mistake when I see a big cheerful billboard, "Arizona – The Grand Canyon State Welcomes You."

Arizona? This isn't where I want to be. This is not where I am supposed to be. This is not what I planned. I'm not even in the right state!

"This isn't really my fault, though," I think, excusing myself from any possible blame, "I was thinking about something important. I just didn't notice."

Then I look down and notice something even more important. My hands are on the wheel. Yup. I'm driving.

So, then, it *is* my fault?

Not so. It *isn't* my *fault*. I'm not flawed or faulted. But it is my respons*ability*, my ability to respond. Accepting that we have the ability to respond to anything and everything that comes our way is seeing our own hands on the wheel and using those hands to turn things around. I am where I am because *I drove here*. Now, I have a choice. Tour Arizona, or turn around and find the right road.

Pathologically positive people feel a sense of empowerment because we know we are in control and able to respond constructively to disaster and discontent.

In agent mode, we accept respons*ability*. We *enjoy* knowing our hands are firmly on the wheel. Even during the initial moment of creative discontent, the pathologically positive don't waste time on blame. Whatever happened, whatever or whoever was at cause, is only relevant as it helps us find the solution. Beyond that, we simply accept respons*ability* to deal with whatever adventure lies in the disaster (like touring Arizona) and enjoy the journey.

Victim mode says, "I can't!"

When asked to do something difficult, unpleasant, or inconvenient, noxious negativity says "I can't."

In victim mode, our job is to find as many reasons as possible why something can't be done. The noxiously negative are habitually certain about this. I say "habitually certain" because they say it frequently and firmly. "I can't do this," "I can't afford it," "I can't handle it." "I can't!"

In victim mode, we don't think much about our thinking as we look at the dark side. It's a habit. It saves us from thinking, trying, failing – or succeeding.

"Oh, Doc, I can't handle that. I just can't. If that happened I would go crazy."

Crazy? Really? That would be interesting to see. Because I'm a shrink, I always inquire enthusiastically about this "going crazy" possibility.

"So you just might tear your clothes to shreds and run madly down the street screaming vulgarities?"

"No, I wouldn't go *that* crazy," they invariably respond.

Shucks. Whatever happened to all of the fun clients?

From a purely psychological perspective, what happens right after we tell ourselves we can't handle it? The next step after "I can't handle it" is, "I won't even try to handle it. I'm done. Finished. Defeated."

"I can't" is a toggle switch on the side of our brain which turns our creative mind off. It is the end of the trail. There is no next step. We are stuck, stopped, finished.

Agent mode says, "I can."

The opposite of "I can't" is obviously "I can." It is followed by an important question, "*How* can I?"

The pathologically positive and the noxiously negative say the same thing, "How can I possibly do this?"

They mean the exact opposite, however.

In victim mode, it is actually a statement disguised as a question. What it really means in victim mode is, "There is no way I can possibly do this." In agent mode, however, it is a real question. "How can I possibly do this?"

The pathologically positive, in agent mode, are well aware that they don't know everything. We may have absolutely no clue about how we are going to answer that question, but we know there is an answer that works, so we ask the question, with full intention of finding the answer – and we generally find it.

Asking the question as a question leads to flashes of creativity and brilliant answers. The more we practice doing this the better, and quicker, it works.

Just as quickly as "I can't" turns our creative mind *off*, "I can" turns our creative mind *on*. It gets us thinking, especially as we ask the important follow up question, "How can I?" This leads to, "How will I?" We then move naturally into actually doing it.

What is the next step? There is always a next step in agent mode. Ask for help, look for resources, consult, question, do something, get it done.

Why do the pathologically positive know we can handle anything? Because, so far, we have. We can handle anything and everything. We always have. We always will. We may not think it will be much fun, but we can and will handle it (and when we do sometimes we may look back and say "Wow, that was actually fun!").

A ten year old client taught me this in a powerful way. He found his parents brutally murdered in their suburban home. A year later, after intensive counseling, and amazing support from his grandparents, he is stabilized and doing well.

I ask him, "What if I asked you last year, before all of this happened, 'Do you think you could handle it if both of your parents were killed?' What would you have told me?"

He responds quickly and vehemently, "No way!"

He pauses for a moment as he realizes something very important for the first time, then says, "But I *am* handling it!"

A ten year old finds his parents murdered, and he is handling it.

Now, what was it you've been saying *you* can't handle?

Victim mode asks, "Why me?"

A little over a decade ago, I start noticing problems with my voice. Gradually, it becomes more and more difficult for me to create the sounds of certain words or phrases. My brain starts talking but the words strangle in my throat. I tell my voice to say something and... zip, nada, nothing — at least nothing intelligible.

Why me? This can't be happening to me. *I can't handle this.* I am a psychologist, an author, a professional speaker. My voice is an important work tool! Communication and conversation is critical to my business. Why is this happening to me? Why? Why? Why?

Of course I don't frame "Why?" as a genuine question. It's a whine disguised as a question.

My excellent pathologically positive advice is for other people.

At first, I assume it has to do with stress. My thriving young practice requires considerable effort to maintain. We are raising four wonderful but normal kids. My wife and I both work and volunteer a significant amount of time in charitable service. There isn't much time for relaxation. It must be stress.

Surely it is not a brain tumor or something equally unthinkable.

Unthinkable? Then why do I think it?

Our subconscious uses our knowledge and experience to propose answers to the "why" question — even when it's a pathetic "whyne" rather than a genuine "why." In victim mode, the reasons for disaster are, of course, disastrous (not opportunities as they are in agent mode). My experience as a shrink, therefore, takes me directly to the most feared conditions in the diagnostic manual.

The condition worsens. The unthinkable keeps being thought. I am quite certain I have a brain tumor.

Why a brain tumor?

Because that's the worst thing I can imagine.

My subconscious elaborates, expands, and magnifies the disaster, then advances to "what next?"

I'll probably die. But before I die there will be chemo, radiation, sickness, baldness, agony. I will suffer horribly.

The voice problem gets progressively worse. My subconscious takes another swing at it. Now my conservative religious training kicks in. This is my fault because I've been bad. That's it! God is punishing me.

The noxiously negative obsess over the terrible injustice and horrible timing of everything that goes wrong.

Of course, while stuck in this mode, we don't realize that if it were *good* timing, it would be neither painful nor difficult. It might be uncomfortable, but mostly a fun adventure with a big "Woo-hoo!" at the end of the experience. Like taking a spectacular spill on a ski slope and ending up in a pile of soft powder – hoping someone got a good photo of it.

While I practice my victim skills, Vicki has a different take on the whole thing. She is fascinated. She is a speech/language pathologist. This is a great opportunity for her to observe a condition she has previously only read about.

She's also becoming weary of the noxious negativity energy-sucking vortex I'm creating around this. She tells me I should see a doctor. I tell her I will get an appointment.

She tells me she already did.

I visit an Otolaryngologist who, like Vicki, is fascinated. He tends to agree with Vicki's theory and refers me to another specialist. I am now locked firmly into my noxious negativity. If this condition requires second and third opinions from specialists, I'm doomed for sure.

I begin to consider who I will ask to be the main speaker at my funeral.

To get the full effect of victim mode, you have to complain regularly and often. It is best to use a whiny voice, with the entire focus on yourself.

Art Berg, a powerful inspirational speaker and author who was also quadriplegic calls us "why-ners."

Mike Schlappi, an Olympic gold medalist in wheelchair basketball, calls us "why babies."

I've been whyning, "Poor me. Why me? Why this? Why now?"

Now I don't even have a voice with which to whyne!

"Why me? Why this? Why now?" are legitimate questions, as long as one is actually seeking real answers. As a rhetorical mantra, however, the questions tend to keep those in noxiously negative mode stuck in the problem rather than moving toward the solution. Our subconscious will accept the mantra whether or not we have a good answer to the question.

The conditioned subconscious default answer to the "why me" question is, "I deserve it. I am a failure. I brought this upon myself." This answer is too often supported and coached by well-meaning parents, partners, even some professionals. "What's wrong with you? You deserve this. You asked for it! How did you attract this?"

The implication is we must be bad, broken, unworthy, inadequate. We are therefore condemned, doomed, stuck.

Agent mode asks, "Why *not* me?"

This is an equally legitimate, but far less frequently asked question. The pathologically positive, like other normal human beings, tend to react to tough circumstances with the same questions, "Why this? Why now? Why me?" But they reframe those questions using their *Pathological Positivity* perception. The questions are similar, but are asked affirmatively — without the whyning.

"Why *not* this? Why *not* now? Why *not* me?"

In agent mode, we answer the "why" question with rational answers after reviewing the circumstances in light of the law of cause and effect, the law of nature, the rules of probabilities and chance, even luck.

Notice, I said "luck" not "bad luck" because luck is just luck, it is neither good nor bad, it just depends on what side of the roulette table you are on.

The Bible suggests that God causes the rain to fall on both the just and the unjust. Even though agents may not immediately enjoy what is happening in the moment, they see luck as universal. It happens to, and for, everyone.

Yes, indeed, "into each life some rain must fall." Thank you, Henry Longfellow. And thank you Ink Spots for setting it to music, which serves to remind us, poetically and musically, everyone gets rained on, whether or not we feel like dancing – or singing about it.

What kind of people get into car accidents? Only those who are intoxicated, negligent, irresponsible? Into whom will those intoxicated, negligent, irresponsible, drivers crash? Other negligent, irresponsible drivers and pedestrians. They will also crash into responsible, sober drivers and careful, observant pedestrians. They will crash into anyone who happens to be in the way.

Again, what kind of people get into car accidents? The kind of people who have encounters with cars. Those who get into cars or walk on sidewalks. That could include you, me – anyone.

So why not? Why not this? Why not now? Why not you? Why not me? You and I are just as qualified as anyone else to get into an accident. "Fault" is essentially irrelevant, unless you are an insurance adjustor. There are good reasons we call such events "accidents" rather than "intentionals." It's no one's "fault." Accidents just happen, accidently. Some say accidents happen for a reason. Of course they do. To give insurance adjusters a job.

So, let's go back to my voice problem.

I am fairly well entrenched in victim mode by the time I finally find a specialist who has seen this kind of thing before.

He immediately recognizes the patterns in my speech to be a neurological voice disorder called spasmodic dysphonia. This is a good thing. Not the condition; but knowing what it is. Just having a name for it creates some new possibilities for me.

Albert Einstein said, "Understanding the nature of the problem is half way to the solution." That makes sense. I can now delete the drama of victim whyning and stop planning my own funeral.

How do I vacate the drama of "Why me?" Deal with reality. Dealing with this condition might be educational, possibly even fun. It has to be more fun than the misery-producing victim-mode perception I was using as a self-torture device.

The specialist says there are approximately thirty thousand people in the United States who suffer from spasmodic dysphonia.

Is that a lot?

I need a dollar bill frame of reference to compare with this tarantula. The football stadium on the nearby university campus holds twice that many, so I imagine the stadium about half full. Wow, that's a lot of people!

A lot of people? Sure, until I spread that number out across the country. If the full stadium represented the entire country, only about three people in the stadium would have spasmodic dysphonia. Hey, I really am special! The reality is, comparatively few people deal with spasmodic dysphonia or even know what it is.

The next question changes everything for me, "Why them?" Why do twenty nine thousand nine hundred ninety nine other people have this condition? I can't make the same arguments I did about me (that they are all psychologically disturbed, deranged or spiritually unworthy of success, happiness, or the right to speak their own language).

I am therefore constrained to change the "why me" question to an easier question, "Why *not* them – *and why not me?*"

This new paradigm changes everything. I have as much right as anyone to deal with disaster. I have equal opportunity to have this challenge. I am just as qualified as the next person to handle spasmodic dysphonia – better qualified in some ways. I have a live-in therapist and, with my extensive education, I can even pronounce "spasmodic dysphonia" (when I can get my voice to work).

Abuse, health challenges, financial circumstances, relationship conflict, or anything else which happens to us or *for us*; notice what happens when we change "why me" to "why *not* me."

Now, true *Pathological Positivity* takes over.

The "not" is dropped and the old question emerges in a new way. The whyne becomes a genuine question: "Why me? Why this? Why now?"

Because. Be-cause. Because of the cause. Cause and effect. Stuff happens. That's all.

By asking the question with a new paradigm, the paradigm of *Pathological Positivity*, we change the perspective and, consequently, the answer to the questions, "Why me? Why this? Why now?" Even if altering our perception does not alter what has already happened, asking "Why" as a real, not a rhetorical whyney question, does alter reality by significantly altering the *meaning* of what has already happened and empowers us to change what comes next into something really great.

Victim mode needs rescue.

In victim mode, we feel the need to be rescued from whatever unpleasant circumstances we are in. In my seminars, I often show a purchased video clip from an advertisement for Becel Heart Healthy Products which features two people going up an escalator. The escalator suddenly clunks to an abrupt stop.

"Oh, that's not good," one says, as the other complains, "I don't need this. I'm already late!" They shout for help.

Their need for rescue echoes off the walls of the apparently empty building. "There are two people stuck on an escalator and we need help. Will somebody *please do something?*"

They sit down uncomfortably on the sharp-edged metal steps of the escalator, woefully waiting for rescue.

A handyman appears at the base of the adjacent working escalator and yells up at them, "Hey! Don't worry about it. I'll fix it in a second." He starts to ride up.

The stranded victims' sense of relief is short lived. There is a resounding "clunk" as the rescuer's escalator also jolts to a stop.

The final scene of this Heart Healthy advertisement shows all three hopelessly trapped and resigned to their dismal fate on disabled escalators (that look curiously like stairs to those of us in agent mode.)

We laugh at the humor of the situation, wondering why these poor trapped victims don't just walk up the steps to freedom.

Silly example? Unbelievable that someone could actually be so caught up in a noxiously negative victim mode they'd actually feel stuck on a stalled escalator? Not so much.

I show this video clip in an executive training with a group of hospital administrators. One of the administrators sheepishly raises his hand to confess that he did almost the same thing.

On his way to baggage claim on a recent business trip, he noticed the escalator was out of order. There was a brief moment of panic.

"Oh, oh! Now what?"

But he, being a successful business executive, arrived at the obvious solution. He looked around for a flight of stairs. There was one a mere thirty feet away.

Breathing a sigh of relief, he headed for the stairs…

Good grief!

Agent mode proactively acts.

Perhaps we are ready for some "Heart Healthy" *Pathological Positivity* solutions in such challenging circumstances. When an escalator breaks down, we could simply use our pathologically positive perception and shift into agent mode. Instead of a warning sign that reads, "Out of Order," broken escalators would have a sign that reads:

> **Escalator out of order.**
> *Welcome to the stairs!*

In the movie *Ever After*, Danielle De Barbarac (the Cinderella character played by Drew Barrymore) is sold to the unsavory Pierre le Pieu (Richard O'Brien) and held against her will. Weary of Pierre's unwanted advances, Danielle takes matters in her own hands and breaks free of his evil clutches.

Meanwhile, Prince Henry (Dougray Scott) learns of Danielle's plight and dashes off to rescue his damsel in distress. His heroic chivalry shifts to comedic awkwardness as he encounters Danielle resolutely striding away from Pierre's property, having rescued herself.

Remember our friends who were trapped on the escalator waiting for the technician trapped on the bottom escalator to rescue them?

Who should their rescuer be?

Remember your favorite Positive Psychologist, driving aimlessly in the desert?

Whose hands were on the wheel?

My dear friend, Mary Louise Zeller, is a sixth degree black belt master of Taekwondo. She inspires hope that there is more to life as long as there is life, as she continues world class martial arts competition at the youthful age of seventy-plus.

As I interview Mary Louise for Live On Purpose Radio[2], I probe to get her take on the escalator syndrome – the tendency to plop down and wait for a rescue. Her response?

"Paul, the troops aren't coming." She pauses to let it sink in. "*We* are the troops!"

In agent mode, we don't wait for the troops to rescue us. We know *we* are the troops! We don't wait for the economy to turn around. We notice our hands on the wheel and turn the economy around ourselves. We don't wait for the repair technician. We turn broken escalators into stairs – and post signs to the world accordingly.

Victim mode creates scarcity.

---

[2] http://www.liveonpurposeradio.com/2009/04/07/living-an-ageless-and-limitless-life/

"Buy now while supplies last! "Get while the getting is good."
"All good things must come to an end."

There is never enough. Never enough good deals. Never enough stuff in your closet or garage. Never enough time, money, love, attention. Those in victim mode operate in a constant perception of scarcity.

We are never even good enough, ourselves.

In victim mode, not only can we never have enough, we can never do enough, be enough. This scarcity focus starts first thing in the morning with a depressed groan, "I never get enough sleep." "I don't have the energy to do this." "I don't have time." The noxiously negative in scarcity mode constantly feel overwhelmed and dissatisfied. They always need more.

Everyone wants stuff – I do, especially on my birthday. In noxious negativity, though, we *need* stuff.

Scarcity perception causes people in victim mode, to grab, hoard, cling to, all they can – sometimes even using people to get stuff –because we can. We are there in force on Black Friday (which is now creeping in on Thursday). We shop in a feeding frenzy, climbing over and pushing others out of the way so we can grab what we want.

In scarcity perception we see a constant diminishment of resources. It will all go away and we will never again have the chance to have what we want.

In victim mode, we not only have a scarcity consciousness, we actually *create* scarcity – for ourselves.

When we buy stuff we don't need just because it is on sale, or supplies are limited, we are likely operating in victim mode with a scarcity mentality.

"Look how much money I saved!"

Don't they mean, "Look how much money I just spent?" They diminished their valuable financial resources by trading it for junk.

Agent mode creates abundance.

In pathologically positive agent mode we not only see abundance, we actually *create* abundance. There is enough and to spare, and there always will be. We know this is true because, if for no other reason, we create it.

Because we live in abundance, we may save wisely, but feel no need to hoard. Agent mode amplifies and magnifies resources, enhancing the realization of abundance.

The pathologically positive sense abundance to the extent they tend to be philanthropists. The pathologically positive have an innate desire to contribute. While in victim mode we use people to help us get things; in agent mode, we use things to help us serve people. We put our resources to the highest and best use, which includes generous contributions to others.

FranklinCovey co-founder, Hyrum Smith, said everything we produce above and beyond what is sufficient for our own needs, is given to us *to bless others.*

The "surplus" abundance is not meant for us to have and hoard but as a resource which *empowers us to serve.*

In victim mode we are consumers.

A few years ago, I'm having dinner with Dr. Jeffrey Magee. He asks me about my business, which at the time isn't doing so well. Jeff gets paid big bucks to consult with big business. This is a great opportunity to get some keen advice from a brilliant man. I'm poised at the waterfall with my little paper cup, ready for whatever wisdom I can receive from this master on the mountain.

He asks several questions, then pauses.

"Paul, you suck."

That's it? I suck? I stare at my paper cup in disappointment.

Dr. Magee isn't playing on words just to be funny. His response is profound and pointed – and dead on target. I am consuming more than I am producing. My business financials prove it. Now I know why I hear a big sucking sound at the end of every fiscal quarter.

The sucking sound is coming from me.

Consistently consuming more than we produce creates scarcity, like trying to fill a tub without the stopper in place.

The odd thing about victim mode is we feel entitled to the things we consume, yet, simultaneously and paradoxically, we feel unworthy of whatever it is to which we think we are entitled.

There is no inherent evil in consuming. We have to consume in order to exist. We consume resources, food, oxygen, space. Sometimes we consume more than usual, like when we are sick or disabled or just in a difficult place. Even in death we at least consume a few square yards of real estate.

What doesn't work is when we regularly and habitually consume more than we produce. In that mode, we are high-maintenance consumers – producing little, taking a lot (hence, the sucking sound).

Sometimes when we are in victim/consumer mode, like I was before I got zapped by Dr. Magee, we don't even realize we are consuming more than we are producing, unless a financial genius or a pathologically positive psychologist gently points it out.

Those who are stuck deeply in this mode don't appreciate that consumption implies the respons*ability* to produce. They may believe they have nothing to offer, and produce no value in this world but they still need to, and have a right to, consume in order to live.

This feeling of worthlessness, strangely enough, actually perpetuates their drive to consume (clothing, cars, commodities, crap) even more than usual. It is a vicious downward spiral.

Most of us have felt it. When we are bored, depressed, not working, we tend to spend. We try to fill the emptiness inside with stuff.

Noxiously negative victim/consumer mode is a killer – literally. Victim mode leads to ever lower self-esteem, increasingly strained relationships, deteriorating health, addiction, depression, suicide, death.

Victim mode transforms the noxiously negative into vampires – the ultimate parasites.[3] When we are around someone in noxiously negativity sucking consumer mode we leave the interaction feeling drained.

In agent mode we are producers.

Producers create more than they consume. Producers create the cars we drive, grow and harvest the food we eat, make the clothes we wear, build the homes we live in.

The next time you go to a store, walk up and down the aisles and think about the producers who made it possible for shelves to be stocked with wonderful products we can purchase to enhance *The Feeling*.

Because producers create more than they need for themselves, there is plenty to distribute to others at a fair price. Through generous choice, surplus is donated as cash, goods, and opportunity, to ease the burden of others.

Producers create profit which in turn creates greater resources and enhances the producer's ability to produce even more; a constant upward spiral of productivity, profit, professional and personal power – and generosity of heart and spirit. *Pathological Positivity* enhances their prosperity, and their power to serve. With *Pathological Positivity*, they create the life they love and a standard of living which enhances life for others.

---

[3] Interestingly, in the 19th and early 20th centuries one in four deaths was due to a disease called "consumption." What's even more interesting is that folklore thought it to be a disease associated with vampires.

Chapter Nine

The Power of Choice
Kleenex and Concentration Camps

What happens to a man is less significant than what happens within a man.
~Louis L. Mann

Viktor Frankl endured one of the most disturbing chapters in our history books. He then re-wrote that chapter as one of the most influential books of our time, *Man's Search for Meaning.*

Dr. Frankl was an Austrian psychiatrist who, because of his Jewish heritage, was arrested and imprisoned at Auschwitz by the Nazis. He was separated from his beloved wife and family, who were eventually murdered by their captors.

Viktor Frankl postulated, and his victorious life proved, that everything could be taken from us except "the last of the human freedoms – to choose one's attitude in any given set of circumstances, to choose one's own way." This profound doctrine that one could choose how one sees things, regardless of how things appear, was born and bred in the black hell of corruption, horror and atrocity known as Auschwitz.

Viktor Frankl knew he could not control his enemies' actions and attitudes towards him, but he could choose and control *his* attitude and actions toward *them*.

He did not choose his prison, but he did choose his perspective – a pathologically positive perspective – and in that moment, he chose freedom – and instantly became free.

What was the choice which brought such freedom? He chose to love his captors. He chose to look past what they were doing and love who they were.

Though he deeply felt the grief, pain, fear of one immersed in the physical pain and emotional and psychological horror of a Nazi prison camp, he chose what we now know as *Pathological Positivity,* manifesting genuine love for everyone – especially those who show up as horrifically cruel.

From a normal human perspective, to remain positive and loving in such a horrifying situation seems illogical, even pathological. From a psychological perspective, however, his constructive response to the atrocities of Auschwitz was not only practical, it was critical to his survival and ultimate success.

This intentionally constructive response enhanced his personal power much more than hate, recrimination, or retribution ever could have. Who is the most immediate beneficiary of this pathologically positive attitude? Himself. No matter the external circumstance, rather than hopelessness or despair, Dr. Frankl's internal feeling was one of living a meaningful life.

If Viktor Frankl can successfully achieve *The Feeling* through the power of *Pathological Positivity* in his extremely desperate circumstances, what does this imply for you and me?

Some of us are as imprisoned by our own thinking as are prisoners behind walls of stone and windows of iron. In fact, to be a prisoner of one's own negative perceptions– though they may seem very real – may well be the worst incarceration of all.

It is also the simplest from which to be set free.

What can you and I do when we are feeling captured, arrested, imprisoned, stuck, overwhelmed? Choose *Pathological Positivity.* This choice is always available to us under any circumstance.

Liberation from one's mental prison requires nothing more than that choice. I say "nothing more than that choice" as though it is easy. It isn't necessarily easy. It is simple, however.

The power to make this kind of choice is, arguably, the main difference between man and beast. Choice is the most important skill we humans have. To choose our position regardless of our circumstances is one of the most important applications of that power of choice. We don't always get to choose our circumstances but we always get to choose our position. We *always* have the power to choose to respond to our circumstances as a free agent in the mode of *Pathological Positivity*.

As we contemplate this idea of making pathologically positive choices especially in really tough situations, it serves us well to consider what we can change or control and what we cannot. The thought is captured in the Serenity Prayer, penned by theologian Reinhold Niebuhr and, in abbreviated form, often repeated as a thematic mantra in Alcoholics Anonymous meetings:

God, grant me the serenity to accept the things I cannot change, the courage to change the things I can, and wisdom to know the difference.

The one thing we generally *can* control is our paradigm — the principles we decide to live by. Then we can change our perception. The combination of paradigm and perception guides our choice about what to do, or not do, about our situation. Do we allow a default (usually negative) reaction, or do we choose a constructive response?

What happens to us is not nearly as important as how *we* happen to whatever happens to us. We have the power to see things how we choose to see them, and make that real.

Friend and fellow speaker, Mike Schlappi, was accidently shot in the chest as a teenager and left paraplegic for the rest of his life. He didn't choose to be shot. He didn't choose the resulting physical paralysis. He did however choose, and continues to choose, his *attitude* about being shot and paralyzed.

Mike makes an important distinction between the common assumption that attitude is how we *feel* about something rather than the actual definition of the word "attitude." In his book, *Shot Happens*, he says it this way:

Every dictionary I have consulted (including a bible dictionary) agrees that attitude is a position. Be it physical or mental, emotional or spiritual, social or financial, attitude is the position that one takes relative to one's situation, circumstance, or environment...

It is the position we take toward our circumstances that turns bad days into good days... Attitude then is much more than mood — it is method. Gaining a better attitude is simply positioning ourselves constructively in relation to our circumstances — and getting back to work — no matter what mood we are in.

Even though we may not be in great mood because of the circumstances we may be in, we can choose a great attitude *regardless* of those circumstances — or the mood we are in. As we choose our attitude or position toward our circumstances, we create how we *feel — a new mood.*

A common saying has gained some popularity among the motivational gurus of our time: "Make it a great day, it's your choice."

Some think it's a motivational mantra which makes life better for everyone upon whose ears it falls. Others feel it is pushy and parental, even guilt promoting. To some, "Make it a great day; it's your choice," is flippantly dismissive of real problems and genuine feelings. It suggests that if you aren't having a great day, it is your fault. If you are in a bad mood, it's your fault because you are choosing to be in a bad mood. If you are having a bad day, it's your fault because you are choosing to have a bad day.

Your car broke down on the freeway and you are late for an important meeting; it's raining on your newly poured cement; your dog dug up your daises; national disaster has struck; you are, for any of a million reasons, in a deep, dark mood; it's your own dang fault — you made it that way — *it's your choice.*

From a psychological perspective, forcing, or pretending to have feelings of euphoria when we are feeling anything but happy is not an appropriate mental health exercise. Skipping about, telling everyone how great we feel when we don't, is a sure way to get rid of excess friends. Lying about how we feel is the low road to insanity which meanders through the valley of depression which is at the bottom of the slippery slope of denial.

However, there is a psychologically sound foundation beneath what these pathologically positive promoters of PMA preach from the platform. When we choose to rationally evaluate our circumstances based on a pathologically positive perspective, and make a logical, conscious choice to perceive *what is* as good, our feelings naturally change.

That is the choice. Not to choose to not have a bad day (gotta love those double negatives), but to choose to interpret what we formerly interpreted as a "bad day" as a "good day."

Look at it this way. Feelings follow attitude – not the other way around. Mike Schlappi makes a strong point that even being rendered paraplegic does not have as much power over his life as does his attitude. He says that making a choice to take a different position and perspective works in 'most any situation 'most any day. He says it is how he shifts his mood from "Crappy Schlappi" to "Happy Schlappi."

Now you know how to pronounce his name.

When we choose to see the good in our bad day and perceive the opportunity within the tough situation, thereby shifting our bad mood into a good (i.e. curious, creative, productive, etc.) mood we then instantly and automatically "make it a great day."

As we choose our interpretation, our attitude (position) toward the day, we automatically govern our feelings about the day. We perceive great big problems as great big opportunities for discovery, growth, invention.

We now perceive our day as great, exciting, invigorating, productive, regardless of its difficulties, inconveniences, even its apparent tragedies. By choosing our perspective, we choose what kind of day it is. Our day *becomes* great because we make it a great day. It is, in fact, our choice.

But, wait!

Before we embark on a quest to seek out and destroy every bad mood that crosses our emotional threshold, let's first decide if there might be a good reason for that mood to be there in the first place.

In her popular book, *The Secret*, Rhonda Byrne describes feelings as our "emotional guidance system." A feeling of discontent, as pointed out earlier in this book, may be telling us something is terribly wrong and needs to be drastically changed, or it might just be telling us things are not how we prefer them to be and can be adjusted and improved.

Is it wrong, then, to feel anger? Frustration? To be in a "bad" mood? We are not wrong to have those feelings — they are simply our system's way of registering discontent. Feelings of discontent are extremely valuable. As suggested in an earlier chapter, it is the rumbling of discontent that accompanies the divine spark, or blindingly brilliant lightning strike of creativity.

We could very well be wrong about our facts, interpretations and perceptions that cause feelings of discontent, but we are not wrong about the feelings themselves. The problem arises when we often interpret our feelings of discontent to mean someone or something *other than us* needs to change: the spouse, the teenager, the boss, the economy, reality, God...

When we insist that something outside our control or power of choice needs to change in order for us to be happy, we feel frustration, anger, resentment. That is when we are well advised to consider a new position — a pathologically positive position — that things are exactly as they should be. If something needs to change, it might just be me.

Debra shows up at my office in a state of panic and meltdown over a recent business failure. She tearfully exclaims, "It's just not supposed to be this way!"

I have a new box of tissues on the end table. In my most sensitive, pathologically positive psychologist form, I empathetically offer her a tissue. As she dabs her eyes, carefully avoiding smearing her mascara, I suddenly slam the box of tissues onto the floor in front of her.

Debra freezes in mid-dab. The sad eyes she was just dabbing now flash with startled indignation (possibly a little fear that her pathologically positive psychologist has finally gone psychotic). She glares at me with an unspoken demand for explanation.

"Well? What's wrong?" I ask calmly. "You don't like them on the floor? Where *should* they be?"

Debra is a savvy, though shaken, CEO. She *knows* the box should be on the side table and not lying on its side on the floor. She also *knows* her business should not be in the tank. She *knows* she is right.

But is she?

The truth is, according to principles and laws of physics and gravity and cause and effect, the box of tissue and Debra's business are exactly where they should be.

As are our lives.

The conditions in our world are orderly and consistent. They conform to natural law. *Every*thing is *always* just as it should be – by law.

Feeling discontent doesn't mean things *should* be different. It means that we *prefer* them to be different. We *prefer* the tissue box be perched nicely on the end table, rather than lying on the floor.

When I launch the box from my hand in a downward thrust toward the floor, the law of physics takes over. The box does exactly what it *should* do and ends up exactly where it *should* be. If we are dissatisfied with its location, we decide where we would like it to be. Then we apply the same principles and laws that got the box were it is, and relocate the box.

The first step in this process is to adjust our attitude and consequently our mood, decide that things are just where they ought to be, and choose where we'd like things to be.

Insisting that things *should* be different brings frustration, and a bad mood.

Deciding that things *will* be different and applying the principles and laws that cause those improvements to come about brings success, and a good mood.

Accepting that things are the way they should be *and* deciding you will change them is not oxymoronic. Both are healthy realizations. Both are necessary for progress.

The pathologically positive person knows it's perfectly okay to be dissatisfied, frustrated, furious, about how things are; as long as that dissatisfaction, frustration or fury is re-interpreted as creative discontent which is the impetus to initiate change.

The law of cause and effect (also misnamed "luck") which has created what is will just as naturally help us create what we decide it will be when we actually decide to implement that change.

Pathologically positive people don't sit around and complain (much). They tend not to waste their time saying, "It's just not supposed to be this way," because they are already making necessary changes so things will indeed be the way they prefer them to be.

We choose to be in agent mode, which guides our perception and attitude about our circumstances. We choose to make intelligent informed decisions as to what to do. We then behave and act accordingly.

Our power of choice is essentially indestructible. As much as life itself, our greatest gift is power to direct life through choice to be the life we love. Even in the most difficult circumstances we always retain that power. We may not have a choice about what happens to us, but, as Viktor Frankl demonstrated in the Nazi concentration camps, we can choose what to do with what happens to us.

Pathologically positive people recognize "the power of discontent." We use it to identify what we can change. We choose to change it. Then we make the change.

This is the process and the power of *Pathological Positivity*. This is the power of choice. This is how you "make it a great day."

CHAPTER NINE

Chapter Ten

Propportunity
Houston, We Have a Problem

To assume without examination that a difficult experience is bad, denies the wisdom of a loving God and the power of the human spirit.
~ Brad Barton

Bad things are bad.

Of course they are. That's why everyone calls them "bad." Our brilliant minds are capable of coming up with a dozen or more reasons why whatever we perceive as bad *is* bad. If we tell our mind to find out why something is bad, it quickly finds ample evidence to support our belief.

Finding evidence to support what we believe, and not seeing evidence to the contrary, is a normal human trait. It is, in fact, the confirmation bias we discussed in chapter seven. Confirmation bias is much more fundamental than simply rejecting data which goes contrary to our bias. It runs deeper than prejudice. Prejudice we are aware of, confirmation bias we are not. We don't even notice, register, or see our confirmation bias. At least not until it is called to our attention.

Our minds have been conditioned to believe that which appears to be obviously true. Bad things are bad. Our parents said so. Our society says so. The dictionary says so. It must be so.

But, again, it's *not*.

In his paradigm shifting book, *Beyond Illusions*, Brad Barton suggests, "perhaps the greatest illusion of all is that bad things are bad. To assume without examination that a difficult experience is bad, denies the wisdom of a loving God and the power of the human spirit."

If you ask Brad how he can be so bold as to say *nothing* is bad, he will tell you that nothing is bad because bad is not a *thing*. "Bad" is an assessment, a judgment of the thing, not the thing itself. Therefore no-*thing* is bad.

If it is true that nothing is bad unless you judge it to be bad, your worst experience can become your greatest experience – provided you decide it is good. Everything, then, must be good – if you decide it is good. In a compelling example from his book, Brad shares the following:

> *It was April 1970. The Apollo 13 mission was in trouble. A crisis jeopardized the lives of the entire crew. The obvious fact was that this was a bad situation. What wasn't so obvious was that this apparently "bad" situation was a call to greatness that was answered by everyone involved.*
>
> *As the spacecraft approached the Moon, at a distance of 199,990 miles from Earth, the number two oxygen tank in the service module exploded, setting at risk the mission and the lives of those on board.*
>
> *John Swigert, Command Module Pilot, immediately contacted Mission Control, calmly under-stating, "Okay, Houston, we've had a problem here."*
>
> *Mission control responds, "This is Houston. Say again, please."*
>
> *Commander James A. Lovell affirms, "Houston, we've had a problem."*
>
> *The oxygen tanks on board the craft needed to be stirred at certain intervals to prevent the oxygen slush from stratifying. Damaged Teflon-insulated electrical wires powering the stirrer motor sparked and the volatile mush exploded, destroying critical equipment and power supplies. The landing at the Fra Mauro Highlands was abandoned and the mission aborted.*
>
> *The complexity of the problem and the immensity of the danger could not be overestimated. The crew and flight control had to exercise tremendous creativity under extreme conditions to jury-rig*

the craft for the crew's safe return. This required considerable ingenuity under incredible pressure while the world watched the developing drama on television.

In the Movie, "Apollo 13," we knew there would be a successful ending because, well, it was a movie. Tom Hanks would surely bring 'em home. But this was real life. There were no guarantees of success. In fact, it is reported that when the President of the United States demanded to know the odds, a ranking NASA official gave the astronauts a dismal one-in-five chance of survival.

That thought was nowhere more poignantly felt than on the spacecraft itself and in the homes of families and close friends of the astronauts.

In the movie that recounted the adventure, when the NASA director lamented, "This could be the greatest disaster NASA has ever experienced," NASA Flight Director, Gene Kranz, refused to see the obvious. He would not even consider the possibility of a disaster.

His response reflects Winston Churchill's comments during the apparently disastrous but ultimately victorious Battle of Britain:

"With all due respect sir, I believe this is gonna' be our finest hour."...

Like Churchill, Gene Kranz didn't just "think positive." He recognized that circumstances which appear disastrous and desperate — even hopeless — could be more constructively perceived as opportunities for greatness. (In fact, you can hardly find an opportunity for greatness that does not at first appear to be a disaster!) Like Churchill, Kranz knew that circumstances do not govern end results; it is our perception of circumstances that governs end results.

With the power of positive perspective, the challenge was met. The NASA ground crew, astronauts, and support personnel looked beyond the obvious and achieved a successful resolution — a victory which proved the apparent disaster was, in fact, "their finest hour."[4]

Pathologically positive folks always challenge the confirmation bias that others subconsciously hold, believe in, and act according to: Bad things are, of course, bad.

But they are not!

It is mid-morning on an uncommonly lazy Saturday and I am mulling over the concept of whether or not bad things really are bad. Are they sometimes bad? Always bad? Never bad? Sometimes good? Always good…?

Suddenly I get a craving for the smell and taste of freshly made, hot buttered bread. I still have Mom's old recipe. It might be pleasant to fill the air with the aroma of home baked bread.

I head for the kitchen and engage in the process of creating a bit of fresh-baked heaven. Halfway through the process, I get waylaid by my daughter, who wants her dad to play a video game with her. The bread raises twice as much as I intended it to and is all over the oven by the time I realize the problem. Irreversible error. This looks pretty bad.

Houston, we have a problem.

As I clean up the mess, Lyndi and Vicki attempt to console me with praise for my feeble effort. They suggest I bake it anyway. At least we can enjoy the aroma and atmosphere it creates as it bakes.

That was, in fact, the original idea anyway, so I agree.

As the bread, if you dare call it such, comes out of the oven, I feel an enhanced sense of disappointment. It is worse than I expected. Yes, this fits well within the definition of "bad". Vicki helps clean up the additional mess.

We sample the ugly twisted fragments. They are surprisingly tasty! Rather than throwing out this apparent disaster, Vicki tucks it away in a Tupperware container. "It does taste great," she says, "let's not just throw it out."

Several hours later, after the initial sting of my failure is gone, I am munching on a piece of my disaster and notice the food dehydrator is now empty of the banana chips I made a few days ago.

Ding!

I grab a bread knife, cut my disaster into small cubes, and arrange them on the dehydrator shelves.

Croutons!

Not just any croutons, but the most delicious croutons you ever tasted. Like the fabled Phoenix, my creation rises from the flames of my oven disaster with a new name, a new opportunity! Bad bread becomes culinary croutons. They were so exceptionally tasty that few of them made it to any salad. Hmmmm...

Bad can indeed be good. It can even taste good! It isn't exactly *Apollo 13*, but those delicious croutons came from, not in spite of, a disaster. It was truly my finest hour — in the kitchen.

These small disaster/opportunities are important. They are God-given rehearsals for the big disaster/opportunities.

As Brad Barton says, opportunity doesn't *result* from a problem, the problem itself *is* the opportunity.

According to my friend Zhu Qin, in Mandarin, the symbols for "problem" and "opportunity" cannot be meaningfully separated. They always appear together.

What if we created our own English word combination of problem/opportunity?

Propportunity.

What kind of shift in thinking do we produce as we incorporate this new word and its meaning into our daily language? It would bring about a simple, subtle, and incredibly meaningful shift in our cultural awareness and appreciation of disasters. What a great step toward reforming our personal, family, community and/or corporate psyche into one of *Pathological Positivity*!

In Shakespeare's words, "There is nothing either good or bad, but thinking makes it so." Sure, experiences can be tough, difficult, painful, life threatening, even life terminating; but *bad?* Not unless we judge it to be so.

But wait, just because it isn't bad, then is it necessarily *good?*

Earl Nightingale thinks so. This father of portable positivity programming promoted the concept of *Pathological Positivity* when he suggested that we react to negative things that happen to us by saying, "That's good," then set our creative mind to work figuring out just what is good about it. This is hardly ever easy.

Are you in a really tough situation? Is it painful? Life threatening? What could possibly be good about that!

That would be a great question, if it were, indeed, a question. Notice, however, there is an exclamation point instead of a question mark at the end of the sentence. That proves it isn't really a question. It's a statement *disguised* as a question. The punctuation changes the meaning to, "*Nothing* could possibly be good about this!" That is our bias. Our experience proves our bias to be true. Negative confirmation bias again takes control and we walk away from a perfectly good propportunity.

Watch your language *and your punctuation*. Try using a question mark.

What could possibly be good about this?

It is now a question – a very good question. It effectively challenges prejudice, conditioned thinking, and confirmation bias. It is perhaps one of the best and most useful questions of all when facing a tough situation.

"What could possibly be good about this?" is a profound question.

The answer promises to be equally profound.

As it is easy for water to run downhill without structure (pipes) and energy (pressure), it is easy for your mind to run downhill in tough situations. "What's good about this! This is tough. This is painful. Painful is bad."

Add structure and energy by asking the question as a question. "What is good about this?" Then, instead of giving in to prejudice and negative confirmation bias, stay in that question until your brain, and the amazing creative mind that operates it, comes up with a legitimate answer.

As we firmly, but kindly, order our mind to do so, our mind will, after some initial resistance, work very hard to find out what is good about whatever "bad" thing we ask it to consider. If that something is painful or unpleasant, it may require our mind to work harder to see it as good. The more painful or difficult the situation, the harder it is to see the good. Yes, that is true, and the more positively life altering it is when we do so.

Our mind is a power tool built to do hard work, and like a well-bred work horse, the well trained mind loves tough challenges. The more we get our minds to practice enjoying tough challenges and seeing them as good, the more it becomes a habit. A powerfully positive, life altering, habit.

Speaking of life-altering, how about situations that are life threatening – like a terminal illness. What's good about finding out that you have a life threatening condition?

Are you asking this as a genuine question?

Knowing what it is puts a handle on the darn thing so you can get a hold of it. Only when you know what it is, can you do something about it. It may not be fun to endure, but it is good to know because the knowing creates possibilities, attitude adjustments, plans, that would not be possible without the knowing.

So it is good that you know. It is good because you can now do something with it or about it. You can seek, find, or create a cure; or write a good end chapter for the story of your life.

So, what *is* good about this difficult, painful, even life-threatening situation? What *is* the opportunity in *this* disaster? Good question, as long as you ask it as a real question. Listen for the answer. If an answer doesn't come, keep asking the question until one appears. Or create an answer. Invite your mind to find, discover, reveal, or create what is good about it.

It works at home. It works at work. Pathologically positive employees are crazy enough to say things like, "The economy may be in the tank, but this will be our most profitable year ever." They then find innovative ways to overlook the confirmation bias that companies generally fail during hard times, note the historical truth that hard times actually tend to make good companies better, and make it happen in their own company.

There *is* good everywhere – even in the most difficult of situations. If we don't see it, it may be because of confirmation bias. Remember, our minds tend to screen out all but that which they are programmed to perceive.

As we get in the habit of assuming and discovering the good of every experience (especially the tough ones) and overcome our confirmation bias to the contrary, we become genuinely, certifiably, *successfully* pathologically positive.

No matter how tough our circumstances, our lives shift and change sometimes imperceptibly, always inexorably, into a life we truly love – not despite the tough times, but because of them.

Chapter Eleven

The Pollyanna Proposal
Corporate Croutons

*...there is something about everything that you can be glad about,
if you keep hunting long enough to find it.*
~ Eleanor H. Porter, Pollyanna

The wildly imaginative producer of really scary stuff, Stephen King, said, "When you're still too young to shave, optimism is a perfectly legitimate response to failure." He is almost right. Fact is, optimism is a perfectly legitimate response to failure at any age.

Innovation and life-improving inventions are generally a result of overcoming or ignoring confirmation bias and appreciating the creative imbalance of life known as "propportunities".

My successful crouton experience from the previous chapter sets us up to consider even greater or more far-reaching and life-enhancing innovations which come from recognizing propportunities.

A notable example is Dr. Spencer Silver, a scientist with 3M. In 1968, Dr. Silver was working to develop new and stronger adhesives. His experiments produced a weak, low-tack adhesive instead. Sometimes characterized as a solution without a problem, Dr. Silver's adhesive was not what the company wanted, and he was reassigned to other tasks. The record of the failure was tucked away in the archives.

Some time later, a creative minded employee named Art Fry attended one of Dr. Silver's seminars where he mentioned the weak adhesive which didn't leave a residue when it was removed. Art spent some of his free time singing in his church choir, but had the annoying problem that his bookmarks would not stay in place in his hymnal. A problem without a solution. So, what good is a weak adhesive?

I can imagine a pathologically positive Art Fry asking the question as a real question as he began to re-think the labeling of the adhesive's characteristic as weakness, "Really, what good *is* a weak adhesive?"

"What if its 'weakness' is its strength?" Art may well have thought. How might this problematic low tack adhesive be useful – and profitable? Art found that a small amount of the shelved adhesive applied to his hymnal's bookmark was just the answer he had been looking for.

As you may have guessed, the answer to that question ("Really, what good *is* a weak adhesive?") became the key to the creation of what we now know as Post-It Notes, one of the best selling office supplies of all time.

The profits from the "Post-It Note Propportunity" made 3M's shareholders very happy. Dr. Silver's big problem was inherently a big propportunity.

Corporate croutons.

Pathologically positive people look at everything that happens – even the most apparently disastrous occurrences – as propportunities. They make a habit of it. Every tough situation is perceived as the potential of another profitable propportunity.

As the promoter of *Pathological Positivity*, I am sometimes accused of being pollyannaish – like Pollyanna, in the 1960 Disney movie of the same name, based on the novel by Eleanor H. Porter.

Is this a compliment or a criticism? I'm not sure, so I rent the movie.

I liked the movie when I was a child. When I got older, I joined in the popular opinion that it was just corny and, well, Pollyannaish. Watching it this time, I pay close attention to Pollyanna's approach to life's challenges in light of my positive psychology practice.

Here is a child who is orphaned, not as an infant, but when she is eleven years old – old enough to understand what is going on. This is difficult and painful. Her father, a minister, had taught her a game to play during difficult or unpleasant times. He called it the "Glad Game." The objective of the game is to purposefully look for something to be glad about in any situation – no matter how tough it may seem in the moment. It is not a denial of the difficulty, but an intentional choice to find and focus on what could be good about it, regardless of how tough it might at first seem.

At first, the townspeople are annoyed by Pollyanna's apparently impractical *Pathological Positivity*.

Stereotypical antagonists habitually cling to their crabbiness, creating an additional challenge for Pollyanna who simply enhances her effort to promote her brand of *Pathological Positivity*, slowly convincing them of its power.

One by one, she inspires them to notice and focus on the positive, and to recognize that such a choice is always available. As the people she touches try on this new attitude, they quickly learn the power of her positive approach to their difficulties. There is a ripple effect as these people start to make a difference for others, and they for others.

They realize that this young girl is on to something.

By promoting *Pathological Positivity*, Pollyanna shifted her entire community's attitude and approach to difficult situations. Before long the entire town is transformed into a mindset of *Pathological Positivity*. In classic Disney style, everything culminates in a happily-ever-after ending as the whole town comes together to applaud their hero.

The character of Pollyanna has somehow gained a negative reputation for being blindly positive, unrealistic, even silly. Being called "Pollyannaish" is not generally a compliment. It should be, however.

Pollyanna did not look at the world through rose colored lenses. She took off the traditional negative lenses and saw the world clearly, as it really is, and chose to deal with it constructively through her exercise of the art and science of *Pathological Positivity*.

In the context of Pollyanna's life situations, she "picked the positive on purpose and by preference from a plethora of possible perceptions[5]" through her father's structured perspective and energy enhancing *Glad Game*.

Pathological Positivity seems indeed "pathological" and impractical, yet it works. The experience of every successful person proves it. Your own success history proves it. Traditional thinking once again is debunked and replaced with something consistent with the truth that every experience, situation, or circumstance is, or can be, for our good and the good of those we influence.

We used to believe in a geocentric universe where the sun rotated around the earth. Copernicus turned the theory around and declared that the earth moves around the sun.

He was criticized by his peers, accused of heresy by his church, but his theory that the earth revolves about the sun, not the other way around, has been proven and is now accepted without debate.

Here is another theory that demands challenge: Success brings us happiness.

Is that really true? It is true that success has long been shown to be correlated with happiness. But does it *bring* happiness? Does happiness revolve around success, or is it the other way around?

In graduate school, a favorite professor of mine repeatedly drummed it into his student's heads that *correlation* is not causation. Yet popular belief has held out that success brings happiness – because successful people consistently score higher on measures of happiness.

---

[5] From Dr. Paul's *Pathological Positivity* keynote introduction. http://youtu.be/Am_K5Cwvrvg

Shawn Achor, a brilliant Harvard educator, lays a firm rationale for *Pathological Positivity* in his book, *The Happiness Advantage*. Shawn cites study after study that convincingly establishes happiness as a *cause* for success. Success revolves around or evolves from happiness, not the other way around. Shawn convincingly demonstrates the same thing that I have consistently observed in my clinical practice. As we improve our happiness through the practice of *Pathological Positivity*, we increase virtually all other measurable indicators of success.

In the words of philosopher Thích Nhất Hạnh, "There is no way *to* happiness – happiness *is* the way."

You've heard the question a hundred times:

"Is the glass half empty or half full?"

If we are operating in noxious negativity mode we see the glass as half empty. It is absolutely true. It is half empty. Of course it is. Any dang fool can see it's half empty. When we are feeling negative, we focus on what is missing and lament the lack of water in the glass.

When we are feeling more positive, we see the glass as half full. Of course it is half full. Anyone can see that. We focus on what we desire, and celebrate the presence of water.

Then there are those who see it as completely full – *all the time*. These seemingly crazy people are not just positive; they are what this psychologist calls *pathologically* positive. *Pathological Positivity* is an empowering mental supernormality that lifts us above the normal perception of "reality." It is a higher level of thinking. We see the glass, and our lives, as completely full – even in the toughest situations.

How is that possible? How can we see the glass as completely full? Must we make up facts to justify our theory – our pathologically positive position? Do we pretend there is more water?

Not at all. We notice and pay attention to what really is – and simply accept the truth. The glass is indeed filled half way with water. It is filled the rest of the way with something just as valuable, and even more immediately necessary to life, than water.

In truth, the glass *is* completely full. The glass is half full of water and filled the rest of the way and to overflowing with precious air.

What if it is lying on its side? What if it is shattered into a thousand pieces? How can it then possibly be full? Because the glass does not contain the air, it is immersed in it. In the same way, our lives are not only filled with opportunity, *we are immersed in such an abundance of opportunity and resources that we cannot contain it.*

Normally, we don't notice the air in the glass — or even around us — because we are used to it. Air is the most immediately important and most abundant life giving substance on earth. We are completely immersed in it. We've never been without it.

We certainly would notice if it was missing.

Shortly before his death from Cystic Fibrosis, my wife's cousin Tyler sat on his hospital bed and watched his brother stand at the window and take a deep, audible breath.

"I wish I could do that," Tyler gasped.

Those who don't have easy access to air notice it every day.

Pathological Positivity enhances our awareness of the opportunities and abundance of this beautiful life, and our gratitude for it.

Pathological Positivity allows us to discover internal power and external resources to achieve the success we desire and deserve.

Pathological Positivity is a genuinely practical approach to finding solutions to every problem. The pathologically positive do not ignore or avoid reality, but intentionally and doggedly insist on widening their view of reality, expanding their horizons, broadening their perspective. They see the possibilities that hide in problems and find or create constructive tools to handle life's inevitable and interesting challenges.

How do we feel when the people around us habitually react to challenges with negativity?

Conversely, how do we feel when their reaction to difficult situations is instinctively positive?

Art Fry, Pollyanna, Copernicus, Shawn Achor, Thích Nhất Hạnh, and the best and brightest of our national and international corporate leaders all have this in common. They see, and focus on, what is rather than what isn't. They see truth, not tradition.

Our greatest leaders know we need uplifting, not downsizing. They do not see problems as "problems" they see problems as "propportunities." These intuitively constructive and creative people already practice the principles of *Pathological Positivity*.

Difficult challenges, even painful disasters, are viewed as propportunities for invention, creation, innovation, and positive change. Energy replaces apathy. Focus replaces fear. Determination replaces doubt. Truth replaces tradition. Productivity replaces lethargy.

Phenomenal prosperity is, indeed, the predictable product of *Pathological Positivity*.

CHAPTER ELEVEN

Chapter Twelve

Surprise!
The Predictability of Principle

Instead of telling our young people to plan ahead, we should tell them to plan to be surprised.
~ Steve Carell (in the movie, Dan in Real Life)

Surprise is one of the most predictable things in life. We are certain our investments will all pay off (because we are special) and we will be financially set by the time our children start leaving home (because we did everything "right"). We are surprised when something else happens.

We think we will have good health our entire life. We are surprised when something else happens. We think our kids will outlive us. But we are surprised. We think our job is secure, and always will be (especially if we work for the government). Something else happens – and we are surprised.

Our nation's economy is doing great, then a couple of misguided political extremists slam hijacked airliners into the Twin Towers and the Pentagon.

We are shocked, amazed, angered, saddened – and surprised.

We plan, prepare, and perform positively, then something else happens. We get to start over. That's life. Being surprised and starting over. Re-thinking, re-evaluating, re-examining, re-discovering, re-viewing. It isn't what we thought it should be, or would be – so we get to think again.

Old journeys end before they were supposed to and new journeys begin before we are ready. The new journey is different than the journey we expected. We are surprised...

...and it can be a pleasant surprise.

With all of life's surprises, what is predictable? What can we depend on? We crave consistency, stability, dependability predictability. It is unnerving to some to realize that change is perhaps the most predictable element of life. What can we do to prepare for this unsettling reality?

We can expect, and plan for, surprise.

We can also plan to enjoy surprise. This we can easily do when we are prepared to deal with it through something just as dependable and predictable as change: The principles and laws which govern success and happiness.

Principle allows us to achieve happiness because of (not in spite of) surprises. Natural law and principle can be depended on with absolute certainty. Proper application of principles assures us great happiness in the midst of great surprises!

What is principle? How does it give us such a guarantee?

During a middle school presentation this spring, a science student defined a theory or theorem as "that which we think is" and principle or law as "that which is." Pretty basic? Yes. Also, pretty brilliant.

Consider the principle of natural attraction commonly referred to as the "Law of Gravity." Do we get up in the morning and muse, "Hmmm... I wonder if gravity is working today?" No, we just put on our shoes and walk out the door assuming, without even thinking, that gravity will be working (we wouldn't need shoes if gravity were not working).

The Law of Gravity never disappoints us. Whatever opposing or changing theories or personal beliefs we may entertain about gravity, contrary assumptions do not alter the principle expressed as the Law of Gravity. It is what it is. What goes up must come down – unless it's strapped onto the back of the Space Shuttle. Of course that's governed by principle and law too.

Apparent contradictions to principle and law are not contradictions at all, but simply manifestations of the balancing or countering effect of other principles we may or may not know or understand.

If you take a flying leap off of a cliff, you fall. Is that a "for sure," or is that a "maybe?" Every time? Some of the time?

What if you don't believe in gravity? What if you think you are a special case and the law of gravity doesn't apply to you as it does to everyone else?

Gravity doesn't care if you believe in it or not – or if you are even aware of it. The law of gravity is a natural principle and governs the end result of your aerial audacity. You will make the exact same splat as believers would. Actually, believers don't tend to jump unless they are harnessed to a hang glider.

Aha! So hang-gliders defy or overcome gravity! No, they don't deny, or defy, the law of gravity; they don't even overcome it, as is commonly said. They use it. Without gravity, hang gliders, birds or airplanes could not fly. If gravity were somehow switched off, a Boeing 747 would become non-navigable. Airplanes need gravity to "overcome" gravity. The law of gravity supports us when we respect it, and drops us on our heads when we don't.

It is, therefore, in our best interest to figure out what principles and laws are at play when we contemplate an important action or make a significant decision like whether or not to jump off a cliff, fly to Paris – or invest our life savings in our cousin's new invention.

It serves us well to conduct ourselves in harmony with principles and laws. Our happiness depends on it. When we understand the principles laws are based on, dots are connected and life (including change and surprise) makes sense.

We have been using the terms "principle" and "law" almost interchangeably. They are not exactly the same, however. Principle is the thing; law is how we explain or apply the thing. Principle is *what is* – regardless of what we think or theorize. Law is how we define or apply principle. Principle is, therefore, inextricably intertwined with law. Law of nature. Law of *human* nature. Laws of science. Traffic laws.

A traffic *principle*, for example, is simply how things work — or don't. An automobile and a locomotive cannot take up the same space at the same time. Trains always win the contest.

A traffic *law* is how we codify the traffic principle in terms of human behavior. "Stop, look, and listen" is the law. It is more than a suggestion. If you don't stop, look, and listen, you will likely hear a rumble, then a loud "woo-woooooo" then a deafening and defining "crash" just before the lights go out and you find yourself hovering weightlessly over your mangled car. Milliseconds later you are drawn toward the heavenly light thinking, "Oh, *that's* what Paul was talking about. Now I understand what he was trying to tell me when he explained the difference between a law (which I can violate and *maybe* get away with) and a principle (which I cannot violate even if I want to)."

"I wonder if heaven allows do-overs?"

When we face a problem, we start with the basic principles as we understand them, then become acquainted with the applicable laws as we work out the details of our plan. If the problem is complex or outside of our field of knowledge and experience, it is usually a good idea to consult with an expert.

Although my dad would never claim to be an expert on plumbing, he has done much more than I have and counsels me on a regular basis when I get into one of my weekend projects. He advised me that there are two basic rules of plumbing.

Rule number one: Water runs downhill.
Rule number two: Don't lick your fingers.

I think Dad was trying to be funny, but in his "rules" for plumbing we see an example of principle (water runs downhill) and law (don't lick your fingers).

Detailed and specific application of principle in plumbing, finance, relationship, business, health, matters of spirit may be best addressed by their respective experts – plumbers, financial advisors, business consultants, medical professionals, counselors. We engage those who are uniquely qualified to assist when our specific need relates to their particular area of expertise because they understand the principles and can articulate the laws that keep us safe and on course to success.

W. Clement Stone's popular mantra, "Whatever the mind of man can conceive and believe, it can achieve" is likely true – as long as we abide by correct principles, apply the corresponding law, and enlist competent assistance as we need it. Whether science or finance or spouse-getting-along-with, we succeed when we apply correct principle. We fail when we fail to do so.

Sometimes we get a do-over. Sometimes we don't.

Amidst unsettling surprise, we can count on the predictability of principle. Principle governs everything. Principle is the cause and effect. Every personal, spiritual, social, physical, psychological outcome or result is governed by principle.

Rather than resist change and insist that things remain the way we thought they should be, when we apply *Pathological Positivity* we anticipate, prepare for, and deal with surprises as a matter of course.

When propportunity strikes, we re-think and start over from where we actually are. Without spending too much time in regret, we get down to the business of creation. Using whatever surprise materials and resources that show up, and applying the correct principles, we create or re-create *The Feeling*.

We love life *because* of its surprises, not despite them.

CHAPTER TWELVE

Part Two

Pathologically Positive Creation

Chapter Thirteen

The Creation of Creation
Assignment of Meaning

What we create on purpose, with Pathological Positivity,
becomes what is. The life we love thereby becomes real.
~Paul H. Jenkins, Ph.D.

The first part of this book is about positive evaluation of *what is*. We focus now on creation of *what will be*.

We have already begun the process of creation by first understanding the principles and process of evaluation. This process of evaluation is how we assign meaning to the events in our life – so we know what to do with them.

In noxious negativity mode, we create a negative meaning for the difficult events in our lives (and we typically try to avoid them).

In *Pathological Positivity* mode, we assign positive meaning to the same tough circumstances (and we typically try to embrace them).

Viktor Frankl suggested that we control our lives as we manage our assessment of our experience and our assignment of meaning. "Life is never made unbearable by circumstances, but only by lack of meaning and purpose."

That is an English translation of something Dr. Frankl likely wrote in German. The pathologically positive translation could be this:

"Life is always made bearable and rewarding by the assignment of positive meaning and purpose to every circumstance."

A graduate school professor told me a story about a small town boy who went to a big city college. My professor heard it from a guy who said he'd heard it from a fellow who claimed the guy who told him about it said his cousin heard it on the internet and swore it was true – so maybe it is.

Randy is from a little town like Bliss, Idaho, home of the Skinny Pig, where I found the dime.

Imagine the culture shock when this small town country boy lands smack-dab in the middle of a college campus bigger than his daddy's farm with a student population five times the size of his home town.

The buildings are impressive, the professors are amazing, the athletic facilities are spectacular, the girls are awesome. It's just a wonderful place.

What isn't so wonderful is how out of place he feels in this wonderful place. As anyone would, Randy wants to feel included. The guys in the dorm are nice enough, but Randy just doesn't feel he fits in. They aren't mean, at least they don't mean to be, but he feels largely ignored. The guys get together in study groups, they double date, everyone plays practical jokes on everyone else – except him.

Randy turns to drinking to drown his sorrows – Dad's Root Beer. It's a little taste of home. Miracle of miracles, he has found a small mom and pop shop just a block away from his dorm that sells it and he frequents it whenever he's feeling down, which is frequent.

One cold drizzly October afternoon, something happens in that little establishment which changes Randy's life.

The entry bell tinkles as he enters the darkened store. "This is weird," Randy thinks, "Why are the lights off? The door's unlocked, but no one's here."

Something moves in the dark. Randy turns, squinting into the shadows as a menacing figure lunges toward him. In one fluid movement, the assailant grabs Randy, spins him around and holds a knife to his throat.

Tune in later for the exciting conclusion...

Don't you hate that? We don't want "tune in next week for the exciting conclusion." We want answers and we want them now! If we can't find an answer, we make one up with as much (or as little) information as we have at our disposal. We assume, extrapolate, interpret, invent and, right or wrong, accurate or inaccurate, we come up with an answer — to *every* question.

Then we assign meaning to the answer.

Then we experience a feeling with the meaning.

And off we go, blithely interpreting and reinterpreting life — usually quite inaccurately.

Whether positive or negative, the important thing to realize is the entire process, our initial perception, question, answer, meaning, and response is driven by our subconscious. Even when we think we are thinking and being quite rationally rational, the process of answering life's questions originates and often remains in the subconscious.

That word, "subconscious," gets thrown around a lot. What does it actually mean? "Sub" means beneath, as in *sub*marine or *sub*way. "Conscious" means aware. "Subconscious," then, means "below awareness."

A subconscious answer is, therefore, an answer we are not aware of (except, perhaps, for the way it manifests in feelings). Sometimes we don't even realize we've asked a question.

We muck about with our subconscious questions being answered by our subconscious mind. Those unchallenged answers create beliefs which drive feelings which elicit behaviors. We act out without ever realizing what we are doing.

Why would we do that? What is wrong with us? Nothing. We're human. That's what humans do. In fact that's what all sentient creatures do. We react without consciously thinking why. It's how we survive (not necessarily how we thrive).

Meanwhile, back at the ranch — or in this case, the mom and pop shop...

In a nanosecond, Randy's subconscious gathers all available facts. Dark room. Approaching figure. Physical attack. Knife. His subconscious perceives, interprets, assumes, extrapolates — and assigns meaning. It asks and answers questions, "What is happening? Why?" It creates meaning, establishes the belief that he is in danger, and reacts to that belief. Adrenaline pumps, heart pounds, Randy freezes.

This is an adaptive survival mechanism. It is a natural way to interpret and respond to the information at hand — especially when there is perceived danger. It makes perfect sense that we do this. It is vital to our survival in the jungle.

Does it work at home or in the office? Not so much. Especially when we are wrong about our conclusions — which we very often are.

Psychologists take great pride in being able to name things. We observe a phenomenon and come up with a name for it. It makes us feel smart. The name we created for the typical mistake we make when we subconsciously answer these subconscious questions is "the fundamental attribution error."

When we observe something happening to others, we tend to over-value *dispositional* factors as the cause for what is happening. When something happens to ourselves, we tend to over-value *situational* factors as the cause.

Kathie sees Thomas stumble over a box left on the floor. Kathie is likely to attribute the cause of this mishap to Thomas' clumsiness or lack of awareness (dispositional). "Watch out, Honey. Be careful," she says sweetly.

If Kathie trips over the box herself, she is more likely to attribute the cause to the presence or inappropriate placement of the box (situational). "Who left that stupid box on the floor!"

We tend to attribute the cause of how we feel to what is going on around us (situational). It is an error to do so. This doesn't mean we are wrong about how we feel, just inaccurate about what is causing the feeling. The actual cause of how we feel is not the situation, but the meaning we assign to it. This meaning then drives our reactions.

If that meaning is subconscious and unexamined and if our reaction is similarly untrained, the reaction can be a liability.

A trained response, however, is an asset — assuming, of course, the response is positive or constructive. Positive? Even with a knife held to our throat? Yes. *Especially* with a knife held to our throat.

This makes more sense as we finish the story.

Paralyzed with fear, Randy's life flashes before his eyes. After two excruciatingly long seconds he notices movement on the other side of the room as a second man rushes toward Randy, grabs the attacker's hand, pulls the knife away from Randy's throat, and pins the assailant to the wall.

As Randy stands there not knowing whether to run, fight, or faint; the two men burst out laughing. They are just a couple of guys from the dorm playing a prank. Randy's feelings shift in seconds from fear to relief, based on his new interpretation of what is happening.

Now his feelings will shift again based on his assignment of meaning to this new interpretation of events. Why are these guys doing this? Are they mean spirited bullies? Are they scaring the living daylights out of him to make him a laughingstock? Or are they finally including him in the group by playing a practical joke on him?

What is critically important to understand, is that Randy's reaction — at least initially — has nothing to do with their intent (he doesn't even know what their intent is) and everything to do with his own assignment of meaning.

The assignment of meaning is what governs his reactions.

Even when feeling relief, the mind still makes that same error of attribution, concluding that we feel the way we do because of what is happening. The fact is, we feel the way we do about events because of our interpretations of what is happening, and our assignment of meaning to those interpretations.

The events themselves do not change. What happens, happens. What is, is. What was, was. What will be will be (que sera, sera). Our perception and interpretation of events and the meaning we assign to the event, however, may change. *That* changes our feelings, which in turn, governs our reactions and responses.

The subconscious process of asking and answering questions is automatic – we can't stop it or turn it off, nor should we. The trick is to make this process conscious, not just subconscious; intentional rather than unintentional.

Most fears are programmed, based on assumptions and reactions, not facts. A young child doesn't know enough to fear a spider or a snake. Toddlers see snakes as something to play with; and spiders as a light snack. When a spider or snake crawls or slithers by, most mothers typically shriek, grab their child, and head for the hills.

Such reactions tend to program the child's subconscious to see snakes and spiders as dangerous. Even as an adult, they will then tend to indiscriminately judge *all* snakes and spiders as dangerous and to be destroyed. In the future, when these fear-programmed children see a snake, they will most likely shriek with anxiety and terror.

The fact is, the great majority of snakes and spiders are indeed dangerous – to flies and mice – but not to humans. In fact, they are an indispensable part of our natural ecology. Through conscious thought and practice we can create a new habit of subconscious thought, and new reactions become automatic.

What if children were not conditioned to fear snakes? Camie, my eight-year-old neighbor, found a little garden snake in her back yard. She convinces her grandma to let her keep it as a pet. She makes a home for it in a terrarium. She feeds it and cares for it. Every day she takes it out and plays with it as one would any beloved pet. She even names it. As Camie shows me her little "Slithy," she makes adoring sounds and tells me how much she loves snakes.

In the future, rather than scream when she sees a snake, she will likely think, "Oh how cute!"

The observable event — a snake slithering along minding its own business — is the same, but individual reactions may be dramatically different depending on previous programming.

Some fear programming may be adaptive. It is not, for example, a good idea to reprogram your pet bunny to regard snakes as buddies. Rabbits are the natural prey of many large species of snakes, so the rabbit's fear reaction is probably adaptive and helps it survive. Unlike you and me, the bunny may in fact be in extreme danger of becoming lunch.

Our physical mechanism is set up to naturally respond to certain stimuli with physiological chemical changes like the rush of adrenaline caused by a sudden drop or a loud sudden noise. Our startle response jolts us to action if there is real danger. This chemical rush can be reprogrammed to be pleasant, which leads to some of us strapping into rollercoasters or dancing in thunderstorms.

We make this process of reaction to our perceived circumstances conscious by intentionally asking and answering different questions, "What does this mean? What *else* might this mean? What if I don't know what it means?

Saying (or thinking) we don't know is risky. When we say it from a position of noxious negativity, "I don't know" is nothing more than a whiney protest. In *Pathological Positivity*, "I don't know" is a statement of truth — an acknowledgement that we don't have all of the data. Then we stay in the question, entertaining a theory perhaps, and continuing to question the theory, even as we respond to the situation. We observe, ask questions, and create what's next.

Reprogramming our reactions gives us more control over creating *The Feeling* regardless of our circumstances. Simple (again, not to be confused with easy), doable and immediately rewarding; this reinforces the likelihood it will continue and become habitual.

Life gets better and better as we reprogram our responses and learn to love thunderstorms, snakes, and surprises.

Chapter Fourteen

Power of Principle
The Trouble with Technique

Success is the predictable, positive result of understanding correct principles – then applying correct technique.
~ Paul H. Jenkins, Ph.D.

David and Brenda have scheduled an appointment for some pathologically positive counseling. They have been married twenty five years. As is the case with many long-term couples, they are on the brink of divorce. There's no real problem. That is the problem.

Brenda declares tearfully that David doesn't love her any more. The magic is gone. The marriage is dead. David counters by telling me (not Brenda), "That's silly. Of course I love her. She *knows* I love her."

Apparently, David is dead wrong about her knowing.

Consider the oft' told story of an elderly couple driving along together in their old Dodge pickup to the country store. Early in their marriage, this weekly trip was an anticipated outing where they would chat happily about the kids, the farm, a new calf. Now, in their later years, it has become a routine journey traveled in silence – a silence that has invaded their marriage.

The wife can't take it anymore.

"What happened to us, Hank? We don't never talk. We don't cuddle. We don't hardly hold hands no more. I don't even know if you still love me."

Hank chews on that for a long minute, then casually replies, "Martha, I told ya forty years ago, the very dang day we got hitched, I loved ya. N'if'n I ever changes m' mind, I'll let ya know."

Martha is not to be dissuaded. She presses, her voice rising insistently, "But, Hank; it jes' don't feel the same. We use to sit close to each other wilst driving to the store ever' week. You'd put your arm 'round me when you was drivin' er hold m' hand." She sighs, "Ah, Hank, it was so romantical."

Hank stares at the road ahead of him for another long moment and finally drawls, "Wa'al Honey, I ain't moved."

Or had he moved? Physically, he hadn't. Emotionally, he had.

Do you want to connect better with your spouse? Much has been written about how to love or make love; holding hands, sitting closer, opening the door for your sweetheart. But that's just technique. If you really want to connect better with someone you care about, learn first the principle of love, *then* go for technique.

Whether you deal with a problem yourself, or with the assistance of an expert, gain first an understanding of the principles involved, *then* the applicable laws – and specific rules, practices, strategies, techniques.

Success is the predictable, positive result of first learning correct principles – then applying correct technique.

I play a numbers game with my clients and audiences. It is a game I always win. I know the underlying principles of the game. I have practiced these principles many times. My opponent typically has not. I win.

I bribe a volunteer from the audience with a free book or CD to play the game with me. I beat them a few times, then ask if they can see what I am doing. They realize I'm not winning by luck.

There is a trick to it. There is a math-alogical principle behind the game, and a technique derived from that principle.

Sir Francis Bacon suggested that "knowledge is power." Actually, effectively *applied* knowledge is power. I understand a correct principle. I learn the correct technique. I correctly apply the technique. I win. Applying one's knowledge of principle and law, through the use of proper technique, is personal power.

If my audience knew what I know, could they win the game? Of course they could. Once they understand the principle that governs the game and apply the correct technique, they too will win every time.

I play this game with my friend and financial advisor, Les McGuire. I show Les the technique so he can consistently win. When he "gets" the idea that "principle governs the game," and I can intentionally set him up to win, he is thrilled. He invites me to speak at one of his financial seminars. He specifically asks me to use this game to demonstrate the connection between applying the principles of *Pathological Positivity* and applying the principles of financial success.

Financial gurus who put on these kinds of seminars command a lot of attention. They drive nice cars, seem to have lots of money, appear to be happy and successful. They seem to have something special going on. People pay thousands of dollars to attend these events so they can rub shoulders with these apparently special people. Participants hope the guru's special something will rub off on them and they too can drive nice cars, and have lots of money.

The room quickly fills with eager disciples. They settle in with pen and paper at the ready to jot down precious secrets for transforming their lives into something they hardly dare dream about.

Les introduces me to the packed hall as "The Shrink Who Expands Your Mind." As their laughter and hearty ovation escorts me to the front of the room, I smile to myself, "Les, I still have a little more shrinking to do with *you*."

I start off my presentation by playing this numbers game. I call up several volunteers who want to try their hand, and quickly dispatch each in turn back to their seats, defeated. This is how many of them are feeling about their financial portfolios.

The audience knows I am up to something; but nobody knows my "secret to success."

"Would anyone else like to challenge me?"

Les is sitting on the front row leaning back casually with a knowing smile on his face. He knows the secret. He has the *technique* down pat. He has the power to win — at least so he thinks.

He raises his hand confidently. "I'll challenge you."

I invite him to the front. I say something profound to the audience about what a smart fellow Les is. We chatter a bit about the relationship between knowledge and power and how Les is confident because he knows the secret to the game. I ramble on about how successful Les is because he understands the game of success. This is, of course, mainly a diversion. I am distracting Les in order to alter a certain factor in the setup of the game. Les is so confident in his ability to win, he doesn't notice *the game has been changed.*

"Les, do you want to start or would you like me to start?"

"I'll start," he responds. He then does exactly what I expect him to do — he applies a tried and true *technique.*

And he loses.

The chuckles rippling through the audience don't do much to ease his discomfiture.

"Play me again," he commands. "I think I know what I did wrong."

"Are you sure?"

"Absolutely."

He loses again.

As Les loses a second time the crowd is more generous with their mirthful mutterings, and Les is more generous with his frustrated face. "I did what you taught me," he queries, "how did you beat me?"

I tell him to carefully look at how I had reconstructed the game.

He spots the change and reacts accordingly, "You deceived me!"

Did I? Did I deceive him? Yes, I tricked him, by altering a factor in the game, but I didn't lie. I did it right in front of his face. It was an obvious change. He just wasn't paying attention. He assumed the game was exactly the same as before, and he faithfully applied the same *technique* I had taught him before — but he failed to apply the correct *principle*.

No matter how perfect his *technique*, he misapplied the *principle* — and lost the game.

Albert Einstein is credited with saying that the definition of insanity is doing the same things over and over again expecting different results.

In a Psychology Today blog post, Ryan Howes addresses that issue by pointing out the distinction between "perseverance" and "perseveration."

Perseverance is steady persistence in a rational course of action in spite of difficulties, obstacles, or discouragement. What drives perseverance? *Pathological Positivity*.

Perseveration, on the other hand, is the persistent repetition of an irrational or irrelevant course of action, which could also include the meaningless or inessential repeating of a word, gesture, or act.

Perseveration isn't pathologically positive, it's just pathological. It is pathological because it is not connected to any cause of any effect. It is repeated just because the patient feels compelled to repeat a meaningless habit.

Success is the predictable positive result of perseverance in applying correct principles, not perseveration in applying techniques which don't work.

I didn't alter the numbers game to embarrass Les. I altered the game to make a point. Les was doggedly doing what human nature tends to dictate. He thought he knew how to win the game because he knew a cool technique. His technique had worked before, so he applied it again. It makes perfect sense for him to do this. It makes sense for any of us to do this. It makes sense, that is, until the game or the playing field changes — which in real life tends to happen quite regularly. Surprise!

The principle behind winning the game never changed. The content and context of the game, however, did change when I altered certain factors. That required a different winning technique.

Principles don't change. Techniques do. Techniques change as situations or circumstances change. Would financial advisors want their people to know that? Would parents want their children to know that? Would employers want their employees to know that? Would field commanders want their soldiers to know that, especially as the enemy — or the weather — changes the game?

Yes, of course they would.

Les wins easily in the next game, and shows his people in a dramatic way to diligently stop, look, listen, and think about the principles involved in challenges and opportunities. As they too apply correct financial principles, and remain wary of trendy techniques, they will win as he just won.

I said I always win this game. Even when I set Les up to win, I win too. We both win because I am playing a different game. My game is to put Les and his people in a position to win by teaching them the principles, not just the techniques, of winning.

The value of distinguishing between principle and technique flips on the light for Les. We take a break from the seminar. Les grabs my arm and pulls me in close — eyeball to eyeball, toenail to toenail. I steel myself for the chastisement I'm about to get for embarrassing him in front of his paying clients. Instead, his eyes twinkle as he whispers hoarsely in my ear, "I'm going to make a million dollars off of this."

I am pretty sure he did. Application of correct financial principles tends to make folks wealthy — in one way or another — sooner or later. Emotional health, relationships, family, finances, career, the numbers game — all are governed, not just guided, by principle. We win as we apply correct principles, even though the end result may not show up until later.

How often do you feel you are winning? In areas where you generally win, you likely understand, or are at least intuitively aware of, the foundational principles behind your success. Consciously or subconsciously, you consistently apply those principles, and you win most of the time.

Our bodies and brains are hard-wired for success. We constantly do "impossible" feats. We walk across the room without falling down. We drink a glass of water without drowning. We successfully breathe in and out every minute of every day. We are actually winning 99.9% of the time.

Kate Adamson's book *Paralyzed but not Powerless* illustrates this point dramatically. After suffering a severe stroke that left her totally paralyzed, she had to learn to do everything all over again. Speak, eat, swallow, stand, walk – everything. We are actually so used to doing the difficult, even the conceptually impossible, we don't realize how successful we really are.

As we expand our areas of winning, we become used to that too. It is one of the beauties of life and success. We get used to it and don't even question what we can do. Success builds on success.

Most of us are painfully aware of other areas in which we do not feel we are winning. In the areas where we are not winning, how likely is it we will start winning by luck?

People occasionally win by luck, but that often gets them into trouble. They think they are good at the game because they are winning but, because there is no understanding of the principles involved in games of chance, their luck eventually turns and they lose again.

They don't build those fancy casinos in Las Vegas on proceeds from winners.

What principles could you learn and apply which would allow you to start winning consistently in areas where you have been losing? As it is with the numbers game I play with my clients, principle determines outcome every time with everything. Consistently. Reliably.

Success may be a game, but success is not a gamble. If that's true, then why isn't everyone successful? They are, if they choose to be.

Earl Nightingale defined success as "the progressive realization of a worthy ideal." "Progressive" in this context means constantly moving forward – proceeding step by step. We start on the path toward our destination. Our journey is successful as soon as we start. We remain successful as long as we stay on the right path (principle) remain aware of, and take advantage of every "propportunity" that arises in our path, and keep putting one foot ahead of the other (technique).

Success, then, is the predictable, positive, *and immediate* result of applying correct principles.

So why was I standing there in chapter one, in Bliss Idaho, staring at a dime on the ground and thinking it was a fortune? Because I had failed to *consistently* apply correct financial principles. The worldwide economic game had shifted and I was focused too much on technique that no longer worked because the game had changed.

Openness to consider our own foibles doesn't come easily or naturally, especially when we suffer from Special Case Syndrome. Observation of principles at work, however, and a willingness to be teachable and open – then applying correct principles through proper technique – is our key to freedom, financial and otherwise.

Understand the principles involved. Learn proper technique based on those principles. Do more of what works and less of what doesn't work. Win.

Chapter Fifteen

So to Speak

Change Your Language, Change Your Life

Time flies like an arrow. Fruit flies like a banana.
~ Groucho Marx

How can you tell where someone is from? Listen to them speak. Much is said in how people speak, so to speak. Texans usually talk like they come from Texas. New Yorkers tend to talk like they come from New York. British talk like Brits. Listen to their tone, inflection, accent, phraseology, use of words, their language. You can tell if someone is a Texan, New Yorker, or a quite proper British lady or gentleman, so to speak.

Does what that little stream is called rhyme with rick or reek? Is the long padded bench-like thing on which you sit a sofa, or a couch – or is it a davenport? Depends on where you come from.

Do you "carry three gallons of water," or do you "cart three gallon of water?" Is it three gallons or three gallon? Do you carry it from the creek or do you haul it from the crick? Do you carry it, haul it or cart it? Depends on where you come from.

Is it "almost right," or is it "just about there," or is it "purt nigh but not plum?" Is it "far away," or "a long ways," or "a fur piece?" Do people fill out a form to finance a farm or do folks fill out a "farm" to finance a "form?" It depends. Are they from northern or southern Utah? Depends on where you come from.

That's how you tell where someone comes from – the words they choose and the way they say and arrange them.

Now, here's a slightly different question. How can you tell where someone is *coming* from?

Listen carefully. Are they speaking positively or negatively, actively or passively, constructively or destructively? Are they expressing what they desire or the polar opposite? You can tell what their position or attitude is about life, other people, themselves, by listening carefully to what they say and how they say it. The words they use and the way they arrange and express them tells you where they are coming from; their "come from," so to speak.

Tone, inflection, phraseology, and word choice reveal religious preferences, political ideologies, racial prejudices, gender bias, and general or specific attitudes about others and themselves.

They tell us if people are coming from a position of *Pathological Positivity* or if they are stuck in noxious negativity mode.

What about you? How do you know if *you* are coming from a pathologically positive or noxiously negative mode? The same way you can tell where others are coming from. Pay close attention to what you say and how you say it, and you'll see very quickly whether you speak the dialect of *Pathological Positivity* or noxious negativity. Just listen to yourself and you can tell where you are coming from, so to speak.

Listen to how we speak and we understand better how we perceive, interpret and respond (or react) to life – and how life perceives, interprets, and responds to us.

Change your language change your life.

Why is it important to know where you are coming from? Because that determines how effectively you will earn the loyal support of your friends and associates; how well you can enlist their support of your ideas, plans, goals, mission, vision.

What earns us the greatest income? What helps us create the best opportunities for ourselves and those we love, find the best employment, form the finest relationships, build a profitable business, create great friendships, be a great political, social, or business leader, a great friend? Our "come from," so to speak.

Paying attention to how we speak helps us respond to life's surprises in a healthier and more productive way. It helps us create effective, constructive, pathologically positive habits of thought which guide our attitudes and actions. That creates a positive attraction between us and the right people. We then help each other create the life we all love.

Change your language change your life. Indeed. It is powerfully true.

Speaking more positively and constructively has an immediate and positive effect on our lives and the lives of others. We feel more encouraged, more productive, more optimistic – as do those around us – which then reflects back to us – and we feel even more encouraged, optimistic and productive. It creates a constantly improving upward spiral. When mistakes are made, we forgive ourselves and others more quickly. This makes it much easier to relax and learn from our mistakes and makes a much smoother transition to improvement mode.

The language of pathological positivity is like the thermostat in your home; it not only reveals, but controls your environment. Setting the thermostat keeps the temperature at a proper comfortable level, and makes your home a better place in which to live.

It is fairly simple, actually quite easy, to speak the language of *Pathological Positivity*.

In noxious negativity mode we say, "I want to thank you."
 In *Pathological Positivity* mode we simply say, "Thank you."

In noxious negativity mode we say, "Don't let me down."
 In *Pathological Positivity* mode we say, "Make me proud."

In noxious negativity mode we say, "We better hurry or we'll be late."

In *Pathological Positivity* mode we say, "Let's hurry. We'll get there on time."

In noxious negativity mode we say, "Don't forget to get the groceries."

In *Pathological Positivity* mode we say, "Remember to get the groceries."

In noxious negativity mode we say, "Stop being so dang negative."

In *Pathological Positivity* mode we say...

Well, we probably smile and don't say anything.

This is no small matter (oops, I mean this is an important matter). Pathologically positive language makes things happen. Ancient Finnish culture called it "Sanan Mahti," or the power of the word. Pathologically positive prayer is communication with the Master of the universe in language that is likely much closer to the Creator's own. According to King David (the guy who brought down Goliath), God is the one who "...spake, and it was done; he commanded, and it stood fast.[6]" That's pretty powerful stuff; no beating around the bush there (burning or not).

In noxious negativity prayer we say, "Please help us that we might be able to be of better service to others." That's like saying, "Help us so maybe we can help if we ever get around to it."

In *Pathological Positivity* prayer, we simply say, "Please empower us to serve others." That kind of prayer gets answered. Guaranteed.

---

[6] Psalms 33:9 – King James Version of the *Holy Bible*

"Wait just a dang minute," you may protest, "most of those things you suggest that people say in noxious negativity mode are things I say every day. I'm not noxiously negative, am I?"

Probably not. The question isn't whether or not you are "noxiously negative." The question is, "What *mode* are you in?" What mode are you generally in when you are under pressure? In which mode do you *speak*? How is that working for you?

The way we speak not only indicates our mode, it also, like a thermostat, determines, creates and controls the mode we are in.

Changing your language and your mode changes your perception of circumstances, and then the circumstances themselves.

Change your language change your life. How much more simple could it be? How we speak is one of the most fundamental elements of being happy, becoming pathologically positive, creating and living the life we love.

George Orwell once said that if thought corrupts language, language can also corrupt thought. He's right. It is also true that if thought enhances language, language can also enhance thought – and if it can enhance thought it can enhance life.

Maybe it could even save a life!

A young couple huddles behind a wall of blackened, twisted steel girders and ragged blocks of shattered cement as war planes roar ominously overhead. Bombs and grenades explode. Bullets whistle past, ricocheting off the cement and steel around them.

Our heroine holds her lover's head in her lap. No, his head isn't severed from his body, he's just wounded; lying there in the rubble, with his head in her lap. He appears to be dying. He didn't expect to die, he didn't want to die, but now dying is all he can think about and he's pretty sure he's about to do just that.

"Oh darling, please don't leave me," our heroine sobs. Please don't die."

Again and again she pleads, "Please, darling, please don't die. Don't die."

What's she talking about?

His death.

So what is he thinking about?

Dying.

Her language is focused on dying. She is hoping against hope he will live — but instead of saying what she'd like, she's focused on what she doesn't want. She's telling him to not die.

And, since he is listening to her, he is thinking about dying.

What's he going to do, then?

Die.

And he does, therefore, die.

Dang.

Great script for a Hollywood romantic tragedy, not such a great script for creating a positive future — especially his!

Speaking in the "negative," referencing what one doesn't like or want or desire is a noxiously negative habit of speaking that has developed in nearly every language system on this planet. It has been a common language default for centuries. This negative default is oft-promoted in books and plays and the dramatic movie scripts of Hollywood — which are then translated in many languages and promoted throughout the world.

The cinema, television, newspapers, advertising, blare at us day and night. Traditional media pumps into our brains a barrage of language laced with scarcity, fear, negativity. A professional newscaster flashes a practiced smile just before announcing the death toll from a pile-up on the freeway. The latest release at the theater is part three of the hit dystopian zombie apocalypse.

A bold sign in a storefront window reads, "Don't miss our sale." Another says, "No waiting." And there's more: "No entry." "Wrong way." "No shoes, no shirt, no service."

In a recent team meeting, I asked a member of my staff if he had accomplished an assigned task.

"No, I got that done right after our last meeting," he replies. Huh?

That's like saying, "No, I agree" or "No, really; that's not a bad idea. Don't you think?"

What are you trying to say? Don't you think? Do not you think? You do not think? Is that not what you mean or is that really what you don't mean?

Speaking in the "negative" or what one doesn't like or desire is a habit of speaking embedded in every language I know of. It represents an ineffective, sometimes crippling, habit of thinking entrenched in our world society.

It's a wonder we manage to do as well as we do in our day and age. Imagine how well we could do, if we simply reconstructed our language a bit?

Shifting our habit to speaking in the positive or constructive *what is* or "what is desired" (rather than "what isn't" or "what isn't desired") is an essential and powerful part of developing a pathologically positive approach to creating the life we love in a world we love.

It is indeed a brave new language for an amazing new world.

Consider the power we release on our planet as we shift social, cultural, national, habits to speak in the constructive tense. Imagine the peace and harmony that fills our world as we communicate with positive images. Imagine the peaceful, prosperous and joyful world we create as *Pathological Positivity* is incorporated into our world languages.

How does this new world look? How does it *sound?* It's quite remarkable, actually. Let's start with common everyday conversations. How do we sound when typical noxiously negative comments and questions are restated in pathologically positive phraseology?

"Don't" statements become "do" statements which get things done. Past and future tense transform into present tense.

"If" is replaced with "when." "When" transforms into "as." "As" morphs into *what is*. *What is* is spoken positively as if it is already a reality; and that *what is* becomes real.

This isn't as strange as it may sound. It's really quite easy and makes a lot more sense as you get used to it.

"When you do..." or "As you do..." is stronger than "If you do." "Do you..." is more direct than "Do you not..." "I think it is..." is more focused than "I don't think it is... "Yes, you are right." Makes more sense than "No, you're right."

"Remember to take your medicine." is much more helpful and likely to be carried out more often than "Don't forget to take your medicine"

"Couldn't you..." becomes a much more accurate "Could you..." "Can't you..." becomes "Can you..." "Won't you... evolves into a more specifically focused, "Will you..." "Don't forget to" becomes "Remember to..." "Don't die" becomes "Live!"

Note the shift from "if" in the following example of a noxiously negative statement evolving into a much more powerful pathologically positive statement:

"If you don't do [important thing], [horrible thing] will happen."
"If you do [important thing], [wonderful thing] will happen."
"When you do [important thing], [wonderful thing] happens."
"As you do [important thing], [wonderful thing] happens."
"Do [important thing] and [wonderful thing] happens."

"Remember to lock the door and take the keys with you when you leave. I love you and I'll see you soon" is much better than "Be sure to not forget to not leave the door unlocked when you leave; and don't leave them in the car either because if you do, you'll lock yourself out and have to walk home in the rain and probably get run over – and I don't look good in widow's black."

In nearly every case, noxiously negative statements couched in what isn't or what isn't desired (won't or don't or can't or isn't) can easily be restated as pathologically positive statements (will or do or can or is).

Which works better, "please don't misunderstand me" or "please understand me"? When you are about to say, "Isn't it great?" (which means, "is it not great" but literally means "it is bad"), say instead, "It is great!"

Which feels better, "don't you" or "do you?"
"Don't you understand? or "Do you understand?"
"Don't you love me?" or "Do you love me?"
"Won't you help me?" or "Will you help me?"

Switch "can't" to "can."
"Can't you decide?" becomes "Can you decide?"
"Can't we be friends?" becomes "Can we be friends?"
"Can't we work this out?" becomes "Can we work this out?"

Now make it clearer and stronger by switching "can" to let's."
"Can we be friends?" becomes "Let's be friends."
"Can we work this out?" becomes "Let's work this out."

Traditional Speech Pattern (noxious negativity mode)	What we really mean (*Pathological Positivity* mode)
Don't stop	Keep going
Won't you please	Will you please
Can't you	Can you
Don't forget	Remember
That's not bad	That's good
No, you're right	Yes, you're right
Don't you agree	Do you agree
I'd like to thank you	Thank you
I don't think	I think
Why don't you	Will you
Don't misunderstand me	Understand me

When we speak in terms of what we want rather than what we don't want, it is easier for the person we are talking with (which may be ourselves) to think through what we really mean.

Imagine wedding vows couched in the negative.
"Do you not take this man to be your lawfully wedded husband?"
"No, I don't not."
"Do you not take this woman to be your lawfully wedded wife?"
"No, me neither."

What kind of lifetime commitment is that? Maybe a lifetime commitment to the funny farm (which, by the way, is a real place).

Listen to most conversations between Hollywood lovers, friends, business partners, partners in crime, outlaws, in-laws, whether in big screen or made-for-television movies. You may notice that the language in the script is decidedly negative; dramatic, yes, often funny, even moving, and mostly negative, much of the time.

As it is in real-life.

And that is a big part of why we struggle so.

It doesn't have to be that way. What if, instead of saying "Don't die," our war heroine pleaded for her sweetheart to live? Might it have added to his longevity if she had said simply and powerfully, "*Live! Please darling, live! Look, there's an aid station right over there. C'mon honey, stand up. Here, I'll help you, we'll get there in a minute and they will help you — Medic!*"

It might have improved his outlook a bit. Certainly it would have enhanced his focus. He might just have focused on living instead of dying, and actually *lived!*

The tragedy would then be a "happily ever after." That would be great. It worked for Walt Disney. He made a bundle in Hollywood!

In the movie *Camelot,* the brave, noble knight, Sir Lancelot, knocks a fellow knight end-over-teakettle backwards off his horse in a friendly joust. The poor fellow lies there in the dust, legs and arms akimbo, in an apparently lifeless pile of chain mail and topped with a dented helmet.

Lancelot leaps off his horse and runs to his fallen friend. He gathers his fellow knight to his breast in a manly embrace and says, "Live!"

Again, with more gusto he cries, "Live!

Finally, with enough power to rattle his comrade's visor, he commands, *"Live!"*

With a shuddering gasp of air, his friend does just that — he lives. Miracle of miracles, *he lives!*

Ah, yes, the power of words — especially those pathologically, positive, constructive declarations of what is or is to be.

What happens to our world society when advertisements, sermons, speeches, motivational and inspirational books are couched in constructive, present tense, *Pathological Positivity*?

Negative motivation (fear of loss) evolves into positive motivation (anticipation of gain). Positive motivation evolves into inspiration (determination to *be* more rather than *have* more). Inspiration evolves into transformation.

We become greater individuals, social energy shifts, the world powers up positively, and we, each one of us, does what every one of us has always said we want to do; we make a difference — a lasting positive change in the world.

We speak that positive change into the world, so to speak.

CHAPTER FIFTEEN

Chapter Sixteen

Wreckers or Builders
The Power of Positive Planning

*Let us not be content to wait and see what will happen, but give us
the determination to make the right things happen.*
~Horace Mann, Education Reformer and Politician

Destroyer or creator. Consumer or producer. Either we practice noxiously negative destruction or we practice pathologically positive production.

> *I watched them tear a building down,*
> *A gang of men in a busy town.*
> *With a ho-heave-ho and lusty yell,*
> *They swung a beam and a sidewall fell.*
>
> *I asked the foreman, "Are these men skilled,*
> *As the men you'd hire if you had to build?"*
>
> *He gave me a laugh and said, "No indeed!*
> *Just common labor is all I need.*
> *I can easily wreck in a day or two*
> *What builders have taken a year to do."*
>
> *I thought to myself as I went my way,*
> *Which of these two roles have I tried to play?*
> *Am I a builder who works with care,*
> *Measuring life by the rule and square?*
> *Am I shaping my deeds by a well-made plan,*
> *Patiently doing the best I can?*

Or am I a wrecker who walks the town,
Content with the labor of tearing down?

~ Charles Benvegar

In our written and spoken word, in our internal and external attitude or position, in our speech, in our behavior, neutrality is not an option. It is like living on two islands in the sea. We may jump back and forth from one to the other, but there is no middle ground upon which to stand.

Walt Disney was one of the most imaginative and visionary creators of our time. After enjoying the enormous success of Disneyland, Walt envisioned another park on the East Coast to compliment the one in California. Walt Disney passed away from lung cancer in 1966, almost six years prior to the opening of Walt Disney World in 1971. When Walt Disney World finally opened, a reporter covering the event commented to Walt's brother, Roy, "It's too bad Walt did not live to see this."

Roy's reply was poignant and clear, "Walt saw it first. That's why we are seeing it now."

Some people say you can't really predict the future. We don't really know for sure what is going to happen, but we predict things anyway. Why not predict things that serve us and others best? In the predicting of the future, we actually help create it. Like Mr. Disney's theme park, we have to see it first in order to intentionally create the life we love. Clarity about what we will create moves us to the next step in our creative process — the plan.

Look around for a moment. Notice furniture, things in the room, structure of the room itself, your clothing, this book. All of this was created. Every creation implies the existence of a creator, a source from which it sprang. The things we just observed first showed up in the mind of their creator.

The very first episode of Live On Purpose Radio was entitled, "Thoughts Become Things[7]." Things don't magically appear, but are brought about through a creation process. Before things show up in the physical world, they are created mentally or spiritually in the mind and thoughts of the creator.

Imagine a cement mixer that constantly and ceaselessly pours out cement. When the cement spills out and onto the ground it makes a random formless mess that hardens and becomes permanent. A cement mixer that couldn't stop the flow would create an overwhelming mass of *something*.

To create something useful with cement, we use "forms." In construction, forms are wooden or metal frames into which we pour the cement. Forms ensure that cement is kept in the shape we want as it solidifies.

Beauty and utility are created when we use forms. In creation, forms are goals, directions, intentions. Forms are not necessary if you only wish to create a mess, although even then you might first imagine the type of mess you prefer.

Mark Sanborn, author of *The Fred Factor*, says, "Everyone makes a difference." People often respond, "Oh, that's a nice sentiment." Not necessarily. What Mark means is that everyone makes a difference – no matter what. We can't *not* make a difference. The question isn't *will* we make a difference, but what *kind* of difference will we make?

This phase of creation requires us to become very clear about how the thing we are creating will look, how it will work, how it will feel, what it will take.

We create the answer to our "if not this, then what?" question in our mind. We speak it mentally or out loud, then we do what it takes to create the "then what" we desire. We do whatever diligence and research is necessary to convince ourselves that not only is this thing possible, but that *we* can,

---

[7] http://www.liveonpurposeradio.com/2007/08/23/thoughts-become-things/

and will, do it. We think it, see it, speak it, plan it, do it – and it is done.

Two decades ago, Vicki and I move our family from Oregon into our current home. Vicki walks through the door into the biggest kitchen we had ever encountered in six years of marriage. I hear her dismayed exclamation, "I hate this floor!"

Who can blame her? It is crummy old vinyl. The kind which never looks clean regardless of how much you scrub it. It curls up on the edges next to the cabinets and looks like someone took sand paper to the high traffic areas.

I don't like it either, but we tell ourselves that we don't have the time, money, or resources to do anything different, so we better just get used to it. And we did. For the next ten years we "got used to it."

There are no time limits for noxious negativity choices. They don't have a sell-by date, the shelf life is indefinite – they just sit there taking up mental space. Finally, after ten years of low grade kitchen floor discontent, we realize we have a different choice – and always have had. We can do something. We can approach this in *Pathological Positivity* mode and make a different choice.

Once Vicki and I make the pathologically positive choice to do something about the floor, we are faced with the obvious question, "*What* will we do?"

You can see how answering this question requires work.

When stuck in noxious negativity, the possibilities are limited because all we see is what we don't want. Mark Twain said, "I can teach anybody how to get what they want out of life. The problem is I can't find anybody who can tell me what they want." We are pretty good at seeing what we *don't* want. That's how we typically think and speak, as we mentioned in the previous chapter. What we're not always so good at seeing clearly is what we *do* want.

What we *don't* want is at the heart of our discontent. What we *don't* want is painfully obvious. What we don't want are the things and situations we call problems. What we *do* want is the creation of solutions to those problems. What we *don't* want is life without purpose or direction. What we *do* want is a life with purpose and direction.

Imagine telling the ticketing agent at the bus station, "I want to buy a ticket, but I *don't* want to go to Los Angeles. I also don't want to go to New York, or San Francisco, or... Well, I just don't like it here."

The frustrated ticketing agent stares at you over his glasses. He has no idea what ticket to sell you. He only knows what not to sell you because he only knows where you told him you *don't* want to be. So he doesn't sell you anything — and you go nowhere.

Get clear about where it is you *do* want to be, say where that is, and the ticketing agent, God, natural law, and many other resources that exist to serve you will happily help you get there.

To answer the "If not this ugly vinyl tile floor, then what?" question, Vicki and I have to do a little diligence and research to see what kinds of options are available.

As we explore new flooring options, we carefully stay in *Pathological Positivity* (what we *do* want) mode rather than getting sucked back into noxious negativity (what we *don't* want) mode. Our mind is fully capable of giving us fifteen dozen things we can't do and an equal number of reasons why we can't do them. At this point in the process, it is not important to know exactly *how* we will accomplish what we desire; we just need to be clear about *what* it is. We first choose our destination. We *then* plan our course to get there.

Vicki and I talk it out and decide we would like a hardwood floor. There, was that so hard? Not when we finally got past what we didn't want.

There is still a long way to go before that goal manifests in the real world, but we are now finally moving forward. The ticketing agent now knows what to do to help us get to our destination.

We often hesitate to ask, and answer, the question, "If not this, then what?"

A couple explains to me all the problems and troubles they are having with their marriage. When I ask what they want, they might respond, "Well I just don't want her to act so irritated all of the time," or, "I don't want him to criticize me so much."

I again ask, "What do you want?"

They again answer by telling me what they don't want. I sit there like the ticketing agent wondering, "Well, what *do* you want? Where do you want to go?"

I keep a small flashlight in my office for the specific purpose of enlightening my clients – and myself – so we can find our way in the dark. I click it on and aim it at the wall so my clients can see the bright spot of light. The light represents what they want. The darkness surrounding this light represents what they don't want.

What would help them see their path better, the spot of light or the darkness surrounding it? The answer is obvious. Once they know what they do want, we are ready to move ahead.

In the same way, the creation process moves forward as we, in a sense, speak our creation into existence with the power of affirmative language that enhances our focus on what we desire, not on what we don't. The more we see what we *do* want, the more we are certain of the direction in which to go – and what we need to do to get there.

By the way, I also have a big flashlight, ten million candle power according to what it says on the casing. The blast of light from that thing is overwhelming. It really illuminates the obvious! I can see small animals on a hillside across a ravine in the middle of the night from my campsite. There is no question what direction *that* light is pointing.

After a decade of recycling our discontent about the floor, Vicki and I finally make the pathologically positive choice to create a hardwood floor in place of the old vinyl. Now we get to create what we want first in our minds. This entails visualizing and then planning how exactly to create the floor; what kind of wood will be used, what color, where it will be, how it will be installed, and, of course, how we will pay for it.

This planning process includes drawing up a floor plan of our house so I can *see* it more clearly. On the drawing, I shade in the area to be covered by the new wood floor. I even use a colored pencil the same shade of the new wood to help me see it in my mind. I get out my measuring tape and jot down dimensions. I calculate the square footage of needed materials. I research online and talk to experts about the process (remember, I'm a shrink, not a flooring expert). I estimate costs and ask Vicki where we will get the money.

All in all, we probably spend a good month or more planning and envisioning the project. In looking back, planning the project was a lot more work and took more time than the actual installation of the floor. I begin to understand why architects get more recognition and pay than the guys who swing the hammers. Planning is a necessary and indispensable part of the creation process. Planning puts the creative into creation. Planning is *work!*

As we do this work, an interesting phenomenon occurs. A sense of urgency builds to where it becomes a driving, inspiring force.

What has changed? We are no longer "used to" the old undesirable state of our kitchen floor. As we visualize and plan for what we would like, what we don't like looks so wrong – so out of place. We talk less about the old floor and more about the new floor. Our language shifts from "if" we get a new kitchen floor, to "when" we get a new kitchen floor. The old flooring isn't supposed to be there, the hardwood floor is; and here it comes!

Consider where you are in the process of answering your own "If not this then what?" questions. Be bold in your dreaming and move forward. See what is to be with your mind's eye. You can create virtually any outcome you truly desire. The "virtual" part comes first.

Are you afraid? What are you afraid of? Inadequacy? Failure? Disappointment? That's okay. In the words of Susan Jeffers, *Feel the Fear and Do It Anyway*. Many dreams die because people aren't willing to do the hard and ultimately exacting work of planning, or they are simply afraid to dream in such detail and ask for their dream to come true – because they are afraid it might not.

Perhaps you feel unworthy of such a goal? That's good. If you feel completely worthy of your goal, you are likely aiming too low. Your dream isn't big enough. Make it bigger, better, shinier, make it more noble more daring; you become worthy of your dream in the process of achieving it.

In this planning stage are at least three major components; seeing, feeling, and believing.

Seeing is the first step in planning. In the words of Michelangelo, "I saw the angel in the marble and carved until I set him free."

I have a circular chain of eight links on my desk that I carved from a family-sized bar of Ivory soap. People ask me all the time, "How did you do that?" A fair amount of technical skill is required to whittle a chain out of a bar of soap, but perhaps the more challenging task is to follow Michelangelo's counsel and *see* the flexible linked chain in a hunk of soap. When people ask me how I did that, I think, "Perhaps a more

relevant question would be, "How did I *see* that?" Seeing is what makes the doing part relatively simple. I simply carve away everything that doesn't look like what I see in my mind.

To create a flexible circle soap

chain, I become a Michelangelo. I sit for a moment without my knife looking over the bar of soap. This moment has to be long enough and focused enough to see the chain hidden in the bar.

Then, with knife in hand and vision in mind, I free the chain.

With regard to my floor; I have to sit for a moment and see the new floor with my mind's eye. When I clearly see what my new floor looks like, it is then a fairly simple matter to proceed. What I don't want cries out to be removed as the clear image of what is coming takes over my vision. With focus and determination, I remove everything that doesn't look like my mind's image of the new floor. That sets the stage for the installation of what I do want.

Whether remodeling homes or improving relationships, what we don't want is relevant, but only to the extent that it helps us see what to remove, demolish, get rid of, cut out, carve away.

We see ourselves interacting positively with our spouse, showing up with confidence for an interview, speaking in positive terms, interacting constructively with our employer and our team, performing beautifully before our audience, receiving the approbation and abundance we deserve. We see it, we say it, we experience it – *then* we do it.

The old behavior that doesn't fit with that image, and the words and emotion that support it, will absolutely and with utter certainty disappear.

Seeing positive outcomes in advance, and thinking and talking as though they already exist (or are about to), sets mind and body on course with success as we personally define it. This kind of plan or blueprint guides the positive construction of our relationships, and creates the life we love.

To help us power up this process, let's get the plan out of our imagination and onto some tangible medium, just as I did when I sketched out my floor plan. Write your plan in your journal. Condense the idea into one powerful descriptive word, sentence, paragraph, and declare, in a written or spoken statement, what it is like, just as if it exists right now.

Paste it on your bathroom mirror or refrigerator or write it on a sticky note and post it on the edge of your computer monitor. Read it out loud at least once a day. Keep the vision clearly in your mind's eye.

What you focus on will eventually materialize.

Goals, mission statements, life vision declarations — written and spoken synopses of our physical plan in constructive, affirmative language — help us envision and ultimately make our dream reality. These are our documents of determination. They keep our vision clear and enticingly in the forefront of our mind. Thus their realization is predicted and assured.

Hold on. We're not done with this idea quite yet. Let's take it up a notch.

Our subconscious attaches itself to ideas or thoughts that are emotionally charged. As we include emotions in our visualized goals and plans, we give our mind the energy to persist through any barrier to completion. The bigger the barrier, the greater the emotional charge needed to project ourselves past it or blast it out of the way.

It's actually pretty simple to do this. *See* the completed project as if it is already real. *Feel* what it will be like to enjoy the benefits of the finished product. Shift from "if" to "when." Think and speak in present tense about the goal. Apply the positive language concepts and recommendations from chapter fifteen.

Project yourself, your family, customers, clients, friends, community, and country into that picture. See everyone enjoying the benefits as your plan becomes reality. Say it out loud in words that assume its accomplishment now or in the future.

This gives our emotional drive sufficient fuel to carry through with our plan.

If the plan is not yet detailed enough, but the emotionally supported "why" is compelling, the "how" will eventually come to mind and to pass. The satisfaction, pleasure, happiness, and peace we create stands in stark contrast to the discontent that started this process off in the first place.

This kind of planning, directed by clear vision and language, and driven with emotional energy, is how we enhance and guide our creative power to create a life worth living and loving.

It is important, of course, to be sure of our direction.

I take a youth group on an outing where we learn how to make and use signal mirrors. These little four inch mirrors are amazingly bright; and surprisingly accurate when aimed properly. We have a lot of fun re-directing sunlight across the lake and around the camp.

Shortly after the youth camp, my boys and I take a hike up Mount Timpanogos, which towers over the beautiful valley where we live. I tuck the signal mirror into my backpack. Playing with it could be a fun diversion during breaks. It could also come in handy in an emergency.

At the summit, the panoramic view of the valley stretching out below us is breathtaking. We pause to drink in the view and some re-hydrating fluid as well.

My brother, Jason, lives in the little town of Midway on the other side of the mountain. I see where his house would be way down in the valley. Out comes the signal mirror. From that far away, I can't see where the spot of light is hitting, so I call him on my mobile phone.

"Hey, Jason! Go outside and look up at Timpanogos."

"Why, what's up?" Jason queries.

"Never mind. Just go look and tell me what you see."

A few seconds later I hear Jason say, "I see the mountain. So? What's going on?"

"Just keep looking." I adjust the aim and try again to zero in on his house.

"I don't get it. What am I looking for?" Jason asks, losing a little patience.

I finally tell him, "I'm up here with the boys and I have this little signal mirror we made last week. I'm aiming it right at your house, can you see it?"

"Dude, I'm not home. I'm in town getting groceries."

The store where Jason is shopping is about five miles from Jason's house. No wonder I missed him. I am aiming in the wrong direction. As I discover his actual location, I make a small, but important, adjustment and zap him.

I am ecstatic. He is mildly amused.

When a gun is fired, where does the bullet go? It goes where you aim it. What if you are not consciously aiming it, or are aiming it at the wrong target? The bullet is still going to where you are pointing the gun. Your life, business, relationships, bank account are all going wherever you are aiming them. Jason "saw the light" as soon as I clarified my direction and aimed the light to where he was, not to where he wasn't.

Planning is aiming and directing the power of our creative energy. By creating in our mind what we desire, and speaking as though it already exists or at least is just about to, we direct our creative power toward manifesting what we desire. We see, feel, believe what we intend to create. The more clearly and positively we see what we desire, the quicker it manifests in reality. As we attain that level of clarity, we create what seems to be miracles.

As soon as I get clear in my own mind about what my kitchen will look like, and aim my thoughts accurately at what I want (not what I don't), everything I need begins to miraculously show up at my house (with a little help from my Home Depot charge card and my Nissan Titan).

All of the materials that now make up my beautiful hardwood floor already existed. These materials sat on shelves and in warehouses, waiting for me to be clear about my plan. It was my clarity of vision of what I truly desired, and my effective work effort driven by a pathologically positive plan for creation, that brought those materials into my house and ultimately made my vision a reality.

We now have for a kitchen floor exactly what we want, not what we didn't.

CHAPTER SIXTEEN

Chapter Seventeen

Dreaming and Scheming
Plan Your Work and Work Your Plan – It Works

People who say it cannot be done should not interrupt those who are doing it.
~ George Bernard Shaw

In 1947 Chuck Yeager broke the sound barrier, proving the sound barrier is no barrier at all. In 1953, just six years later, Scott Crossfield flew at Mach 2 – twice the speed of sound. Then Chuck beat Scott's record again.

Mankind has now managed to propel a human being through the air at speeds many times the speed of sound – and we still refer to it as a "sound barrier." Barrier? Is it? As it turns out, it is no barrier at all.

How fast can a human being go on foot? On May 6th, 1954, Roger Bannister achieved the impossible when he ran a mile in less than four minutes. Actually it wasn't impossible, it had just never been done before – not that we know of – so it was generally *believed* to be impossible.

That's almost the same thing, but not quite.

Roger Bannister's time was 3:59.4 – three minutes, fifty-nine and four tenths of a second. Such a feat had never been officially recorded prior to that time. Until this time, popular medical opinion suggested that the human body was not physically capable of running a sub-four-minute mile.

Many referred to it as the four minute mile barrier. Like the sound barrier. Was it really an actual barrier? How would such a barrier look?

You are trotting along at a healthy quarter-mile-per-minute pace, about fifteen miles per hour. Then you figure you can actually run a little faster and break a world record; so, on the last lap, you boost your speed about a quarter second per minute faster.

You are about to break the four minute mile speed record when – wham! A big brick wall rises up in your path and smacks you in the face, preventing you from completing the feat.

Wow! There really is a four minute mile barrier!

Silly? Of course. And that's the point. Most barriers are silly imaginings of limiting habits of thought.

We have learned from elephants that our barriers are typically mental, not physical barriers. They are conceptual figments of our imaginations established by habits of erroneously limiting thoughts.

You have likely heard that circus elephants can be controlled by conditioning them from their youth to accept imagined, yet strongly believed limitations. The biggest elephant in captivity can be held fast by means of a relatively light chain fastened around its leg and secured to the ground by a small stake, like the ones used to secure the circus tents and awnings – if they believe they can't break their bonds.

Here is this enormous, powerful animal held captive by a puny, insignificant little chain attached to a small stake driven into the soft earth.

Why does he not just walk away, breaking the chain or dragging the stake along with him? Because the chain and stake are not actually insignificant; they represent daunting limitations to the elephant – mental limitations, not physical ones.

Captive elephants are trained as calves to stay put when restrained in this manner. The little ones cannot escape. They may try with all of their might, but can't break free, so they eventually stop trying.

Powerful adult elephants are more than strong enough to break the chain or pull up the stake and be free; they just don't know it. They remember the futility of trying to escape, and simply have stopped trying. Even if their limitations once made sense, they are no longer real.

I have been told that, when commanded to do so by their keeper, these elephants will pull up the stake with their powerful trunks, move it to another location, and hold it there while their tender pounds it into the ground. They are then stuck in the new location.

Are we like the elephant? Are we held in captivity by bonds we could easily escape if we just realized we could? Do we stake ourselves to a spot and stand there stuck just because someone told us — or we told ourselves — we are stuck? Do we accept limitations as barriers impossible to overcome, like the sound barrier or the unbreakable four minute mile barrier?

The entire concept of "impossible" deserves some re-thinking. Through his public speaking and inspirational writing, Art Berg inspired millions to take on impossible tasks.

Having become quadriplegic from injuries sustained in a car accident, Art accomplished "impossible" tasks every day: brushing his teeth, putting on his socks, getting into his wheelchair. The title of his book, *The Impossible Just Takes a Little Longer*, is a reflection of the motto of the Army Corps of Engineers in World War II, "The difficult, we do immediately. The impossible takes a little longer."

What keeps you from reaching a dream you hold dear? What is your barrier? A lack of resources? A broken system? Personal criticism? Professional opposition? Intimidating circumstances? Crushing physical or spiritual burdens? Limiting beliefs? Whatever keeps you from your goal is a "barrier" that blocks your way, making your personal dream the impossible dream.

Such a barrier may not be a barrier at all. It may actually be a milepost along our path. Perhaps it is a guide whose very existence, even its resistance, lets us know we are on the right track.

In the movie *Harry Potter and the Sorcerer's Stone*, a giant three headed monster-dog named Fluffy is kept in an isolated part of the academy. Why is he there? To guard the treasure — the coveted and much sought after, Sorcerer's Stone.

Of course, until now, no one has a clue where the stone is. They also don't know why Fluffy is there. Then Harry and his friends put two and two together. Fluffy is guarding something. He is blocking their path to something valuable. Fluffy is there because the Sorcerer's Stone is there.

Aha! So *that's* where the treasure is!

If Fluffy hadn't been in the way, Harry and his friends would never have recognized the path to their desired treasure.

Discovering things that are *in* our way proves that we are *on* our way. The very fact that a giant barrier stands *in our path* indicates that we are *on the right path* — to something important. It may even be that the more valuable and important our goal, the bigger and more daunting the barrier.

In his book, *The Dream Giver*, Bruce Wilkinson defines the barrier as a giant — a completely overwhelming obstacle in our path to whatever is important to us. This giant, like Fluffy, is standing in the way of that which we are on the way to.

Looking past the obstacle and focusing on what we are on our way to, serves us well in getting past what is in our way.

You've heard the classic story about the Philistine giant, Goliath. Historians estimate that Goliath was somewhere around nine feet tall. Two feet taller than NBA star, Shaquille O'Neil, Goliath was indeed a formidable foe. He threatens and intimidates the entire Israelite army. No Israelite soldier dared go up against him. He was a menacing bully, a giant human barrier standing in the way of victory.

According to archaeologists, the average Israelite soldier in those days was somewhere around five feet six inches tall. Goliath was almost twice the height and probably three or four times the bulk of the average warrior.

Israel's fighting machine was a force to be reckoned with; nevertheless, the army of Israel cowered before this monster of a man.

Remember Aragog, the "giant" spider in chapter five? Giants like Aragog and Goliath are only giants compared to something smaller – like a five and a half foot Israelite soldier with a two foot long sword.

Enter David, a young shepherd boy with a care package for his big brothers. David sees this giant mocking and bullying his brothers and their friends. He gets a little hot under his collar.

"Who is this to defy the God of Israel?" David demands incredulously. Driven by indignation, this shepherd boy volunteers to face Goliath.

David isn't a burly, battle-hardened warrior. He isn't even in the army. He's probably still a teenager – too young for the draft. David is likely no taller than about five foot two. The top of his head might reach Goliath's belt buckle. So, what is David thinking?

He's thinking past the Giant. He's making a different kind comparison than the one the soldiers have been making.

In analyzing this giant barrier to success, David doesn't compare himself to Goliath; David compares Goliath to God. In comparison to the creator of the universe, the earth, and a bunch of really big dinosaurs, Goliath shrinks in David's eyes to the level of pipsqueak. It's kind of like comparing Aragog, my big hairy spider, with my son who helped me catch him.

Putting things in their proper perspective puts David in position to effectively challenge this human wall standing in the way of victory. Driven by indignation, fueled by faith, sparked with the power of his vision and his faith in his God, this small shepherd boy with a sling shot, and one well-aimed stone actually *runs* out to meet Goliath. Add the speed of a four minute miler to the speed of a stone released from a sling. That stone's velocity roughly equals that of a ball fired from a military musket...

And another giant barrier bites the dust.

Now, to be fair to Goliath, David wasn't just an ordinary little shepherd boy made soft from lolling about day after day in the sun with nothing else to do but watch a bunch of cute little lambs frolic in the field. He was a pretty tough cookie. He had already dispatched a bear and a lion he caught nosing around looking for lamb stew with shepherd pie for dessert. And he was a pretty darn good shot with that sling.

Still, compared with Goliath, David was laughable as an opponent, especially when the Philistine army had Goliath's back.

On the other hand, compared to God, the mighty Goliath was laughable as an opponent, especially when The Force was with David.

David's vision of victory, fueled by faith, was bigger than the giant barrier standing in his way. He kept that vision clear, became worthy of that vision in the process of its realization, and the giant went down hard, clearing the way for victory.

When we shrink our giant barriers down to size by comparing them to a dream or goal that is much bigger, we put ourselves in position to take them on and take them down. What we focus on is what makes the big difference.

Steve Brady is CEO of Brite Music Company in Salt Lake City. He is also quadriplegic. Like Art Berg, Steve faces giant barriers in doing things that are relatively easy for you and me. While interviewing him for a talk radio broadcast, I ask Steve, "How do you do it? How do you stay focused on the positive, while struggling with such overwhelming obstacles?"

Steve replies, "You have to look past the bug guts."

"Look past the bug guts?" This philosophy is new to me. Steve explains. When driving, bug guts sometimes get splattered all over the windshield. It is easy and somewhat of a reflex to focus on the disgusting splotches left behind. When we do this, what happens to our vision of where we are going? It gets blurry. When we look past and through the bug guts to keep a clear vision of our goal, the splatter becomes unnoticed, irrelevant.

When we are focused on bug guts on the windshield, we are not focused on the much more important destination. Tiny splotches of bug guts get in the way of what we are on our way to.

If all we can see is the stuff that splattered all over our life and dreams of success, then we need to look past the bug guts and see clearly what is out there beyond the splatter.

About six weeks after Roger Bannister accomplished the impossible by breaking the four minute barrier on the mile run, his new record was broken on June 21st by Australia's John Landy.

How is it that a barrier considered by many to be impossible to break could be broken by *two* different people in one summer?

The *standard* now for the mile run, in order to truly compete at a world class level, is less than four minutes. As of the original publishing date of this book, the world record for the mile run, set by Hicham El Guerrouj of Morocco in 1999, is about seventeen seconds faster than Roger Bannister's "impossible" performance.

When we pull up the stakes and chains that restrict us, other elephants see that they are capable of the same. We don't just break our barriers and achieve our impossible dream, we free those other powerful folks who work with us, associate with us, look to us for leadership, to break their chains and move past their barriers.

In chapter ten, I shared an excerpt from *Beyond Illusions*, written by my friend Brad Barton. Brad is more than a phenomenal author, speaker, and magician who knows how to look beyond illusions. He is a barrier breaker.

In March 2013, Brad joined the ranks of Roger Bannister and John Landy by also breaking the world record for the mile. In this case it was the masters division – for old guys like Brad and me. The previous record was 4:20.18 set by John Hinton in

2008. Brad came in at a smoking 4:16.83. That's like finishing twenty two meters ahead of John Hinton, if they were physically in the same race. I'd say more about Brad's world record breaking quest, but he keeps breaking other records so fast I can't catch up with him.

Taking down giants like the master's mile is not something you do just because you are fast. In the months of training for, pursuing, and finally breaking this record, Brad also broke his foot and cracked three ribs. It would be easy to get discouraged from the pain and travail of attempting the impossible – and quit trying to do what has never been done.

By the way, when Chuck Yeager broke the sound barrier, he was also suffering from broken ribs. Brad and Chuck both looked past the pain and saw a vision that was bigger than their giant barriers, bug guts and broken bones.

Seeing and feeling the accomplishment of our goal lead us to believe in its possibility. Planning and preparation enhance that belief. When we embark on this creation process, whether it is relationships, or finances, a new kitchen floor, or a new world speed record, the thing we are about to create doesn't yet exist in the real world. That's because we haven't yet created it.

As creators, one of our primary tasks is to see, and believe in, that which we are about to create; and speak of it as though it exists already – or is about to.

Yes, it is normal to have doubts. It's also sensible to replace doubt with faith and belief. As much as our own fears and doubts and negative phrasing are the primary barriers to creating amazing miracles, our beliefs in our dreams and our positive phrasing is the primary barrier buster.

In his famous recorded message, "The Strangest Secret," Earl Nightingale suggests the power of this choice. He compares the mind to a fertile field, ready to receive whatever crops we are inclined to plant. If we plant corn, the field will produce corn. If we plant nightshade (a deadly poison), the field will produce nightshade. The field will produce exactly what we plant. We plant belief, we reap faith. We plant faith, we reap positive action. We plant in our fertile mind a clear vision of what we are creating, and our mind will, in time, return an abundance of what we plant and nurture.

There are two important reasons for us to see past the bug guts, take down our giants, and make real our dreams. One is we get to enjoy our dreams. The other is when we realize our own dreams, we open the door for others to do the same. We begin to truly love the life we live *and* we inspire and empower those around us to live the life they love.

Choose to believe in the creation of your dream like you believe in gravity. Keep your language constructive. Look past the bug guts and keep your vision clear. Your dream will very likely come true.

CHAPTER SEVENTEEN

Chapter Eighteen

The Power of Practice
From Fault to a New Default

Without Goliath, David is just some punk kid throwing rocks.
~ Billy Crystal in the movie My Giant

You are driving along a winding country road on a sunny winter day minding your own business. There is a steep wall to your left and a sheer drop off to your right. You look out over the valley, drinking in the beautiful snow frosted view. Suddenly, you find yourself driving into a hairpin curve. You are going too fast! You slam on the brakes and your car begins to slide toward the edge of the cliff.

What do you do? Step harder on the brakes and steer away from the cliff edge? Ease up on the brake and steer toward the cliff?

You have no time to think about it, mull over your options. You don't even have time to decide. Your brain will do it for you. Right or wrong, it will do what you taught it to do – a long time before this emergency arose.

You are piloting a small fishing boat in the Pacific Ocean about thirty miles offshore. An unexpected storm charges in from nowhere, slamming into you with winds at sixty knots.

What do you do? Turn and outrun the storm? Open the throttle, bring your boat about, and point your bow into the storm?

You don't have time to consider your options and decide what you'll do. Your brain will do it for you. Right or wrong, it will do what you programmed it to do – a long time ago.

Default reactions are automatically programmed into our neural pathways. This reduces the thinking load during our response to emergencies, as well as when performing daily mundane tasks.

We put commonly repeated responses on autopilot. Again, this may be unintentional (passive experience) or intentional (habitual practice).

When you walk into a room, you don't have to think about the myriad of complex physical tasks required to be in precise coordination in order for you to do so without falling on your face or ramming into the door frame. Your brain automatically puts the mundane tasks of keeping your balance or shifting your weight into neural pathways, so you don't have to think about it every time.

In corporate trainings I sometimes have participants race against each other to see who can type their name the fastest. Seems like a simple task right? Probably whoever has the shortest name wins, right? Not necessarily so. The better typist? Rarely. Why? As you likely suspect by now, I've tossed a monkey wrench into the works.

Generally when you type your own name, you don't even think about the letters because you have programmed your mind to automatically go into autopilot as soon as your fingers touch a standard computer keyboard. A quick sequence of highly coordinated, well trained, deeply conditioned finger movements and, voila! Your name magically appears on the monitor.

In this race, however, my willing subjects get to use non-standard keyboards I provide. On these modified keyboards, I have scrambled the letters and numbers, assigning them new locations on the board.

Imagine typing your name on my special keyboard. For most of us there is an initial reaction the more brilliant psychologists refer to as the "Oh Crap" reaction. This reaction occurs at the precise moment our mind connects with the surprise and realizes, based on the circumstance before us, the old neural pathways are no longer effective in producing the desired result.

Is it even possible to type our name on a scrambled keyboard? Of course it is. It just takes more time and effort than normal. Can we become proficient in using that modified keyboard? Likely, yes — with practice.

Why would we want to? We already know the standard keyboard, and it is designed to be efficient with the language to which it is keyed.

Even if the standard keyboard wasn't more efficient than a randomly scrambled keyboard, years and years of conditioning to the exact same input producing the exact same results in the exact same situation have programmed, bone deep, our neural pathways.

Significant, meaningful, repeated behaviors get programmed into a neural pathway, an automatic circuit designed to save our poor, overworked brains from the arduous task of thinking through every single thing we do every single time we do it.

Our brain creates these neural pathways automatically and naturally. Learning to speak and spell, singing old tunes, walking, typing, riding a bicycle, and choosing, or getting used to, paradigms. We do it again and again, then eventually we think, feel, speak, and do according to our programmed neural pathways.

Neural pathways. Autopilot of the mind. Our brain's cruise control. This mental autopilot leaves the brain free to think about unexpected, novel or more important things, like analyzing the life lessons taught by the hit television series, Duck Dynasty.

There is a down side, however. Our autopilot also sometimes gets us to do and say things that get us in trouble. Because most of what we do is a programmed reflexive response, we sometimes react in ways we're used to, but don't always serve us or anyone around us.

Right or wrong, we have already practiced our responses to common situations. These programmed reflexes take over. The result is not always pretty.

There is an upside to this downside. We can change our neural pathways just like we can learn to type on a new keyboard. This may not be particularly easy because of our pre-existing neural pathways; but with repeated practice, any destructive-reaction neural pathway can be reprogrammed to produce, just as automatically and mindlessly, a more constructive reaction – a pathologically positive programmed response.

This certainly does require some work; but it certainly does work!

Charlie Wakamatsu, founder of N.O.V.A. Principles[8], is a retired police officer with a bit of a competitive streak. During a recent business trip, Charlie asks if I'd like to go bowling. Sounds like fun, so I agree. Charlie decides to make it more interesting, which means there's a bet involved. He proposes that the loser buys dinner.

It's a pretty safe bet – for him. He's a fairly regular bowler. I, on the other hand, have been bowling maybe five times in ten years. So, yes, I'm probably buying dinner.

A few frames into the first game, I notice things are not going so well – for him. They are, however, going remarkably well for *me*. I finish the game with my all-time high score which is a solid thirty points better than my previous personal best.

"I thought you said you haven't been playing," Charlie challenges.

"I haven't," I reply defensively, "I haven't bowled in…"

Then I realize I *have* been bowling – on our Wii game system. I didn't think about that when I said I hadn't been bowling, because it is just a video game I play with my kids on a television in our living room. The virtual game, however,

---

[8] www.novaprinciples.com

apparently provided repeated mental practice that transferred surprisingly well to the real game.

Charlie buys dinner.

The victory rings somewhat hollow, though, because we are on the same expense account for the trip.

Why did I expect my bowling skills to deteriorate without real practice? Because that's what normally happens. Unless there is some force to the contrary, Mother Nature's default is downhill. Mountains erode, buildings crumble, roads deteriorate, bridges eventually collapse. Rain falls, hits the ground, and flows downhill.

This is good. If water didn't flow downhill, we'd never get rain and it would be pretty much impossible to irrigate the veggies growing out back. Water follows a course of least resistance down through a hoed row in a garden then down to a lower row, and so on. On its way *down* the row, water sinks *down* through the soil to the roots of the plants.

But what if your garden is uphill from the water source? How do you get the water to flow up? Change the default. Apply constant positive pressure to reverse the default and elevate the water. Water will flow uphill when we use metal or concrete pipes or otherwise contain it, and with positive pressure move it in a new direction.

Elevation requires lift. Lift requires positive pressure. Sustained positive pressure will get water to flow uphill. It's the same with our marvelously malleable minds. Sustained positive effort will create the changes we need.

Consider the following mental metaphor.

As water which flows downhill without direction and pressure to do otherwise, our default reaction to life's propportunities generally takes us downhill. Without intentional choice and mental practice our emotional reactions to propportunities is typically, or at least initially, negative.

How do we advise? How do we argue? How do we lead? Our default is to find fault and it is all downhill from there. How do we change that default? With understanding, and positive intention, we can reverse it.

But it typically won't last. Making the positive choice is one thing. Doing it habitually is yet another. We'll soon default again to the downhill unless we do something to capture the new default and set it in concrete.

Simple? Yes.

Easy? Not so much.

Like learning to use a whole new keyboard, changing our default requires lots of practice. Through intentional, repeated practice of *Pathological Positivity*, a new habit is created, a new default is set, a new language is spoken, and our conditioned response – our default position – becomes a practical programmed proclivity for positivity.

Repeated practice provides the structure and energy required to make permanent this positive change in our approach to life and its challenges – a *habitual* response of *Pathological Positivity*. The affirmations embedded in the Pathologically Positive Prescription at the end of this book provide such structure and direction. Intentional language, repeatedly practiced with constructive focus and positive intent, provides the pipes and pressure to change our default from downhill to uphill. Once this emotional infrastructure is set firmly in place through constant practice, your mental and emotional plumbing problems are over.

Viktor Frankl said, "Between stimulus and response there is a space. In that space is our power to choose our response. In our response lies our growth and our freedom."

Even in a knee jerk reflex response there is a moment between the rubber hammer strike and the kick – a moment between the experience and the reaction. The knee jerk isn't really a response, it is a reaction – until it is purposefully chosen and trained. Normally, our default actions are mindless, generally defensive, typically negative reactions.

Through programmed practice, thoughtless unintentional reaction becomes thoughtful intentional response. Through further practice, the intentional response becomes a new (this time constructive), "reaction." A new default has been set.

What new responses can we practice so that *Pathological Positivity* guides our response in life's tough surprises? Examples of how to use *Pathological Positivity* have appeared throughout this book. You might recall from chapter ten that one of these techniques is to say, "That's good," even if circumstances don't seem to be. Sure, we can force ourselves to say this, but it seems unnatural, awkward, and even wrong — like typing on a scrambled keyboard. For it to become a natural response requires emotional acceptance of the truth of it, improved language, and repeated practice.

Let's try a few on for size. Start with any circumstance that troubles you. Think about it for a moment. Now say "That's good."

Bankruptcy? Pause. Think, "That's good."
Divorce? Pause. Think, "That's good."
An affair? Pause. Think, "That's good."
A debilitating illness or injury? Pause. Think, "That's good."
A heartbreaking loss? Pause. Think, "That's..."

Whoa! Back up the truck. These are clearly *not* good!

At least it *seems* they are clearly not good. The reaction that these difficult or painful situations are not good makes perfect sense, like steering away from the direction of a skid, or turning your back on a storm and running away.

Now, metacognize (yes, it's another new word). Think about your thinking. Pause. Think. Watch what your mind is doing. Through intentional metacognition, you will notice the internal conflict which comes up when you imagine an incredibly painful situation and then steer into it or otherwise face it head on by saying, "That's good."

In this exercise, "That's good" is not a moral judgment. It is more of an affirmation of a starting point from which we move forward. Perhaps it would help if we changed the statement "that's good" to a question: "Is there anything good about this," or more directly, "*What* is good about this?" And "what is good" is not really about the thing, it is more about the fact that you are experiencing it. What is good about that?

Make sure you keep the question mark firmly in place.

"What is good about this?"

This is an honest question. It is also a great question. It is open to possibilities. It doesn't force your thinking, but it does help you challenge your old approach to life's difficult situations – pleasant things are good, painful things are bad. This is a logical approach that has always seemed "right"; however it did not help you face tough situations as well as you could and deal with them as constructively as you can.

Reactions which seem counterintuitive at first can become programmed pathologically positive responses. Novice drivers naturally turn their car's wheels away from a skid on a wet highway surface. It seems the right thing to do, but it doesn't work. It sends their car into an out of control spin. Turning your wheels in the direction of the slide, seems wrong, but it works.

It feels completely counterintuitive when you are first instructed to do this, until you actually do it a few times. Then you find that it works. You maintain control and are more likely to pull out of the slide safely. The more you practice handling a skid this way, the better it works.

Soon, it becomes intuitive. A positive reaction that works has replaced a negative reaction that doesn't work.

Experienced sailors know that when a storm hits, you bring your ship about so the bow faces the storm, rather than giving in to fear, turning tail, and running.

Turning into the direction of a skid, turning to face the wind and waves during a storm. Both seem counterintuitive – yet they both work. Our new conditioned response to turn and face a challenge, looking for what is good about it and the propportunity in it, works much better in dealing with disaster than our original knee jerk reaction to turn away or even run from it.

The greater the difference between the negative default reaction and the pathologically positive choice that must be programmed into our mental and emotional hard drive, the more difficult the work. That *is* good because, generally speaking, the more important the challenge, the harder the work; the harder the work, the greater the strength and ability that is developed.

The Biblical David wouldn't have been famous had he prevailed in a fight with someone his own size. In the movie *My Giant*, Billy Crystal put it aptly, "Without Goliath, David is just some punk kid throwing rocks." The giant illuminates the hero's greatness.

CHAPTER EIGHTEEN

Chapter Nineteen

The Power of Work
The Means to the Miracle

I am a strong believer in luck, and I find the harder I work the more I have of it.
~ Benjamin Franklin

Another law, a law of physics, states that matter cannot be created or destroyed, it can only change from one state to another. Nothing is created ex nihilo (from nothing). Everything has to be made from something by someone.

Remember my new kitchen floor? I said all of the materials that now make up my floor miraculously appeared in my home when I became clear about my plan. It seems like much less of a miracle, however, when I clarify that my truck and a trip to Home Depot were required as the actual means to the miracle. Your mind naturally goes to this step when I tell you the stuff showed up. You ask yourself, "*How* did it show up?"

The "how" is the power of work.

Once I became clear about the way the floor would look, what materials were needed, where it would start and end, how much it would cost, and every other detail I could reasonably anticipate, I started to move the elements and reorganize the stuff. I began the actual physical work.

I engaged my boys, my neighbor, and my dad to assist with this project, because those piles of materials that showed up at my house just kind of sat there until we put our hands to work. As much as this step may seem obvious, sometimes we overlook the fundamental necessity of work.

I sometimes recommend *The Secret* to my clients, a movie based on a book by Rhonda Byrne. The movie helps them wrap their minds around the power of choice and the power of planning. The movie does a great job of depicting the importance of those two particular steps of the creation process.

The movie is far less clear, however, about the power of work. In one scene, a young boy very clearly holds in his mind the image of a bicycle. He thinks about it, imagines it, cuts out pictures of it. Then one morning, he opens his door and there it is. The bicycle has miraculously appeared!

What the boy and we, as viewers of the movie, don't see behind the scenes is the work done to bring the "miracle" of the bicycle into the boy's life. Positive imaging alone was not enough to bring the bicycle to the boy, it required some work. Work – ours or someone else's, or both – moves us past frustration into fulfillment and satisfaction. It is the means to the miracle.

To manifest great things we must do a little more work than we may have anticipated, but less than we fear.

Remember, stuff just sits there until you move it. Water runs downhill until you add pipes and pressure to alter its course. Cake ingredients are just ingredients until someone mixes and bakes them.

There is no substitute for good old fashioned *work*. Professional titles are often actually named after the work activities they represent. Cooks, bakers, farmers, painters, builders, receive their titles directly from the work they do. Teachers teach, runners run, writers write.

I have held this book in my mind and heart for more than a decade. The reason you now hold it in your hands is because I went to work, put my hands to the keyboard of my computer, and physically wrote the words. As I go to work and write, my thoughts become the book.

If something *works* keep doing it – if it doesn't *work* get rid of it. This includes thoughts, feelings, behaviors, and attitudes.

Work makes things work.

In addition to the obvious necessity of work in the creative process, consider also the importance of work in creating, developing, or repairing our own mental health.

"Not working" is a phrase we often use to mean "broken." It is no wonder that a person's self-esteem and sense of purpose are hit so hard when they lose their job or retire and consider themselves as "not working." When people are not engaged in productive work, they are more likely to become depressed, anxious, and dissatisfied with their life.

Russ is a convicted felon. After his release from prison he finds it difficult to get a job. This is a tough situation for him because one of the main requirements of his probation is to go to work and maintain full time employment.

He tells me how frustrated he is with his situation. He wants to work. He needs to work. He is entirely capable of working. But no one will hire him.

I ask him if he is working.

He responds in frustration, "You aren't listening, Doc. I just told you nobody will hire me!"

"Yes, Russ, I heard what you said. No one will hire you. I get that. But that is not what I asked. I asked you if you are *working*."

As we continue this discussion, Russ realizes there is an abundance of work he can do. He may be unemployed but that doesn't mean he has to be unoccupied. He chooses to be occupied, beginning immediately. What is his occupation? Work.

He decides to work full time, whether or not anyone hires him. As soon as he takes this position with regards to occupation, he sees many opportunities for work. A lawn needs mowing. He mows it. A garage door needs realigning. He realigns it. A child's bike needs fixing. He fixes it. He picks up trash, paints fences, fixes more things, mows more lawns.

He weeds flower beds and gardens. He mows again the lawns he mowed last week.

Russ improves and maintains the look and feel of his own neighborhood by providing service to others. He gets paid, sometimes with cash, sometimes with an invitation to a family dinner, sometimes with a smile of gratitude.

He performs full-time work as he continues to look for full-time employment. Russ transforms his surroundings and his own mental health. He becomes less depressed and frustrated, more enthused about life and its possibilities.

Russ eventually does get a job, *after* he starts to work.

A close friend of mine did the same thing as Russ. He once ran afoul of some pretty nasty folks who did not appreciate his speaking up for others. His big mouth got him fired and, worse, the employer blacklisted him. Illegal though blacklisting is, the employer who fired him did everything he could to keep my friend from finding a job.

My friend went to work anyway.

He did exactly what Russ did. He found work that needed to be done, and did it; whether he got paid or not. He worked three days a week doing yard work and other odd jobs, and three days a week creating a new business focused on helping others in similar circumstances as he had been in.

He was told he could not succeed because he was not properly qualified. He succeeded anyway. Why? He went to work, even though he was unemployed.

Today, over three decades later, my friend is an international expert at the occupation he created by simply being willing to go to work even though he was unemployed.

Booker T. Washington once said, "No man, who continues to add something to the material, intellectual and moral well-being of the place in which he lives, is left long without proper reward."

Some work is more productive and meaningful than other work. You might go into an empty lot and spend the whole day moving rocks from one side to the other and then back again. While it would be a lot of work to do this, it probably serves no useful purpose other than to exercise your muscles.

Then again, one never knows.

In the Disney movie, *Holes*, the boys at Camp Greenlake are required to dig holes every day because they are told it "builds character." It doesn't. There is no purpose for the boys except grueling mindless busywork; they are bored, defocused, unenergetic. The superintendent, however, has a clear purpose. She is actually using the boys' labor to help her find a buried treasure.

How energetic do you suppose the boys would have been had they known that they were digging for treasure?

When there is clear purpose to the work, or when that purpose is revealed, work takes on meaning and energy. The stronger and clearer the "why," the more easily the work is sustained.

Benjamin Franklin said, "I am a strong believer in luck, and I find the harder I work the more I have of it." I agree. The harder I work, the luckier I become. I love my life and I love my work with others to live on purpose. A client comments, "Dr. Paul, you are so lucky to have a job you love."

Luck? How can it be luck when I created this? The elements that I rely on to create are there already in abundance. For everyone. In that regard, yes I'm lucky because I had the opportunity to create this wonderful career I love, which like my life, I create on purpose. I get to work with others to live on purpose the life they love. How lucky can I get!

Thoughts become things. All of the steps that we have covered so far culminate in manifestation, which is the observable product of our work. The ideas in our mind show up as real things in the physical world we get to touch, enjoy, and share with others.

How lucky can *you* get? What do you desire most? What is your purpose, your goal, your mission, your dream, your vision? Get clear about what it is you want to make real. Reset your defaults. Go to work. Manifest those realities as concrete outcomes in your life.

You will be one of the lucky ones.

CHAPTER NINETEEN

Chapter Twenty

Pain Pushes, Pleasure Pulls
Either Way, We Move

As we adjust our perception and realization of our own discontent,
we get leverage on ourselves to actually make the changes we've
been promising ourselves to make.
~ Paul H. Jenkins, Ph.D.

One of the most common laments I hear from clients is, "Why do I do what I do, when I know what I know?" An oft repeated parable suggests an answer:

Every morning in Africa, a gazelle wakes up. It knows it must run faster than the fastest lion or it will be killed. Every morning a lion wakes up. It knows it must outrun the slowest gazelle or it will starve to death. It doesn't matter whether you are a lion or a gazelle: when the sun comes up, you'd better be running. [9]

I would actually prefer to use the metaphoric *cheetah* and gazelle comparison. Lions aren't all that fast, but the cheetah and gazelle are both smokin' fast! Not sure who would win in a footrace — which the gazelle and cheetah run nearly every day; one to eat gazelle steak to live and the other one to live to eat salad.

Now, whether we are gazelle or cheetah depends on our mode. Noxious negativity mode has us running in fear — eyes

---

[9]An early published instance of the parable appeared in the *Economist* magazine in 1985 in an article titled "Lions or gazelles?" The quotation is credited to a securities analyst named Dan Montano.

set wide like the gazelle to see behind us. We talk scared, we act scared, we are scared. *Pathological Positivity* mode has us eagerly running toward our goal eyes set like the cheetah's to focus forward.

The direction and speed may be the same, but the feel is very different. One mode is moving toward what we desire; the other mode has us running away from what we fear.

Not to disparage the gazelle. He can't help it if he's a vegetarian.

As you know, pleasure and pain (actually the gaining of pleasure and avoidance of pain) are primary motivators. They both represent discontent.

The experiencing or anticipation of pain and the desire to relieve or avoid pain represents one side of discontent — the side that pushes us away from something.

The desire for and experience or anticipation of pleasure represents another side of discontent — the side that pulls us toward something.

The anticipation doesn't have to be for or against something specific, initially. It may be as simple as a desire for something better than what currently is.

Pleasure and pain push or pull us toward moving or not moving, toward change or staying the same. There is always some degree of both pleasure and pain whether we make positive changes or stay stuck.

<u>Staying Stuck</u>   <u>Positive Change</u>

Pleasure   *Pain*
of staying stuck   of staying stuck

Pain   *Pleasure*
of getting unstuck and making   of getting unstuck and making
positive changes   positive changes

We have a natural, neurophysiological instinct to seek pleasure and avoid pain. This hard-wired instinct moves us either direction on the continuum, because we get pleasure and pain both ways. It is the classic approach/avoidance conflict. The pain of Harry Potter and his friends having to deal with the three headed monster-dog, Fluffy, guarding the treasure vs. the pleasure of owning the treasure. Two forces pulling or pushing us in opposite directions.

Pain may manifest as simply a threat of pain. Pleasure, likewise, may register as simply anticipation or hope of pleasure. As long as the monster dog's threat of pain is, or *appears* to be, greater than the pain of not having the treasure, we are unlikely to go after the treasure even if it is really awesome.

Will we change or not? Will we go for the pleasure of the treasure or back away from the pain of dealing with the dog?

We often desire change and even promise ourselves we will change. Why do we do what we do, when we know what we know? Will we *start keeping* those promises we make to ourselves, or will we *keep starting* to keep those promises? The answer lies in our perceptions of pleasure and pain.

Join me in a counseling session with Anna. In fact, let's counsel her together.

Anna is a mother of three pre-school children. She is depressed and lacking energy. She is a good mother. She desires to be a better mom. She figures that getting through this depression will help her accomplish that.

After some consultation, all of us agree that in order to consistently feel better, Anna must exercise regularly. Clinical studies bear out that physical exercise is generally more effective than antidepressant medication in alleviating depression and restoring healthy emotional balance. We, therefore, challenge Anna to exercise three times a week.

She stares vacantly at us for a long moment. Then with an audible sigh, her shoulders slump and she stares down at her feet. Her response is barely audible, "Yeah, I know I should do that. Okay. I'll try."

Her words said "yes" (actually a listless "yeah") but what does her language tell us? Will she? Will she actually try? What do you think the chances are she will actually do it? Zip? Zero? No way? Snowballs have a better chance on a Phoenix sidewalk in August!

Anna's hesitant, noncommittal verbal and body language reveals her perception of the pain in dealing with the barriers between her and the almost impossible hope of better energy and a happier life. She perceives the barriers as pretty great — and pretty real. She has to get someone to watch the kids, get dressed, go to the gym, pay the fee. The anticipated stress and weariness of exercising, and then the ensuing soreness, is greater than her perceived pain of not having the treasure (which she is not confident she can really get anyway).

The thought of not getting her treasure is also unpleasant, but at least she is used to that disappointment.

The known pleasure/pain will, therefore, win over the unknown pain/pleasure because fear of the unknown is generally perceived to be greater than fear of the known.

Adding to our challenge in helping Anna, is the fact that depression has a nasty side effect that actually makes it harder to do the very things that will help her the most. It pushes the pleasure/pain continuum even harder toward staying stuck.

You and I have our job cut out for us in inspiring or motivating Anna to commit to a program of exercise.

Anna's pleasure/pain continuum looks like this:

Staying Stuck

Positive Change

Pain
of exercising

Pleasure
of exercising

Hard work
Boring workout
Too much effort
Have to get up to go
Gym fees
Find a babysitter
Sore muscles
Nothing to wear
Takes time

Relief from depression
Better health
Increased energy
Manage weight
Feel good
Fitness and vitality
Better mom
New outfit
Improved marriage

Pleasure
of not exercising

Pain
of not exercising

Easy
Comfortable
Can keep avoiding
No immediate costs
Get to indulge self
No accountability
Excuse to be lazy

Miserable
Depressed
Lack energy
Weight fluctuations
Out of shape
Feel terrible
Relationship damage

Anna is stuck in a common deception. She has great reasons to change. She has the ability to change. Life will be so much better when she changes. She knows it.

So why doesn't she change? Why is she stuck? She's in a trap. It's actually a mind trap or maze — a mental labyrinth that keeps her turning in on herself. Part of that is the depression itself. Depression is a mental/emotional/physical state where it feels much more comfortable in the moment to stay rolled up in a ball with the covers over one's head.

Another part of Anna's trap is her *perception* that the pain of change is greater than the pain of staying stuck. There is, in fact, no immediate perception of pleasure of change — certainly not enough to outweigh the apparent immediate pleasure of staying in the warm dark place, however dangerous and destructive it might be. Though there is an idea of pleasure that would result from positive change, it seems too distant and delayed. Too hard to imagine.

Still another part of her trap is her self-talk. The way she perceives, feels, and talks about herself and her fear and her stuck-ness.

For her to get unstuck, Anna needs to be very honest and clear about her discontent — her pleasure and pain.

When she looks closer, she will realize that the pleasure of change is far more valuable and real to her than the pleasure of not changing. She will also realize that the pain of not changing is far greater and much more real than the pain of change.

The mind trap is affected by timing. The main psychological barricade to Anna's changing has to do with *when* she gets to experience the pleasure and pain.

Staying Stuck	Positive Change
Most of the pain from positive change comes **NOW** – on the front end of the change.	Most of the pleasure from positive change comes **LATER** – after the change.
Most of the pleasure from not changing comes **NOW** – we currently enjoy the comfort of avoidance.	Most of the pain from not changing comes **LATER** – we know the pain will hit, but not necessarily today.

Anna perceives *now* pain to be greater than *later* pain, and *now* pleasure to be greater than *later* pleasure. She perceives it not by actually thinking it through, but by default. This is the psychological hurdle Anna must clear in order to actually keep those promises she made to start exercising and make other positive changes.

Let's release Anna from the trap.

We ask Anna to get out her checkbook and write a check for a thousand dollars. Anna looks at us as if we just asked her to let her toddler play on the freeway. It is nothing more than a mental exercise in discontent, but we have her attention.

She cautiously plays along. "What are you talking about?"

We explain that her promise is to exercise for at least thirty minutes three times a week for three weeks.

We promise to hold her check for now. We will set up another appointment for three weeks out. We further promise that if she keeps her commitment to exercise, we will return her check. If she does not keep her commitment, we promise to cash her check and use it at our discretion, but not toward her account.

At first, she refuses to do something so silly as to write a check. It's too risky. Then she realizes there is no risk at all, as long as she does what she says she will do — which is perfectly doable.

She gets it. She realizes the check is simply a way of emphasizing and bringing into immediacy the pain of not changing — the painful discontent of staying stuck in the muck.

She writes the check.

She instantly feels better because, while she already knew she *could* do what she needed to do in order to be a better happier mom, she now knows she *will* do it. Her confidence in herself increases. Not confidence in her ability to do it — she already had that — now she is confident she *will* do it.

She smiles as she writes the check. Her smile broadens into a grin — the first sign of spontaneous emotion since she began her counseling. Even her language changes.

"You do know you aren't cashing that check don't you!" She declares. It is definitely a statement disguised as a question. This time, it's a good thing!

In writing the check, Anna slams shut a back door she has always slipped through in the past when she promised herself she would exercise. As she locks the back door locked with a thousand dollar lock, she knows she has nowhere to go but forward. Anna always wanted to go forward, now she *wants* to go forward times a thousand dollars.

For the next three weeks, Anna exercises just as she says she would. Her feelings of confidence and positive physical and mental energy increase exponentially. Her confidence increases, her language shifts, she changes. She becomes who she really is.

What really changes for Anna is her *perception* of pleasure and pain. The pain of not changing was already very real and getting worse; still, the perceived pleasure of staying stuck kept her from doing anything about it, regardless of how simple and doable she knew it was.

The pleasure of positive change is real but seems vague and distant. One thousand dollars artificially enhances the pain of not changing and puts immediacy into the decision to do what she already knows how to do and already wants to do. When she becomes clear about that pain, she changes. She has to. She can't afford not to. She can no longer stay stuck. And like a truck stuck in the muck whose wheels finally find solid ground, she lurches forward and is soon humming down the road toward her brighter horizons wondering why she didn't get started sooner.

Her outlook changes, her energy changes, her language changes, and soon she encourages others to come along on the journey with her.

Anna improves her life as a result of her positive change. In fact, change is immediate (and improvement is imminent), as soon as her *perception* changes. As we adjust our perception and realization of our own discontent, we get leverage on ourselves to actually make the changes we've been promising ourselves to make.

A little push *at the right time and in the right way* and the little bird who wants to fly, can fly, who teeters on the edge of the nest boldly chirping it's declaration to fly, actually flies. Promises kept. Affirmations declared. Steps taken. Depression down. Energy and confidence up. Success!

Are all clients motivated in the same way as Anna? Of course not. People are motivated, inspired, and transformed by different things at different times in different ways for different reasons. The principles are the same, but the specifics can vary greatly. For Anna, a lightning bolt of possible pain (losing a thousand bucks) enhanced the possibility of pleasure of getting past her depression and being a better mom. It helped her get moving.

For others, a bright flash of clearly visualized potential and anticipated pleasure may be the motivation. The discontent that gets some going may be seeing and noticing the unfulfilled needs of others, a family member or friend, a business associate, their social group, or society in general — and the potential benefits to their friends or their society that success will bring.

One of the most important jobs of a counselor is to help the client decide what will help most to get them moving initially, and what will keep them in positive motion. What motivational or inspirational idea or transformational principle will work best — and at what time, and in what order.

Not to compare my clients with stubborn livestock, but the challenge is similar to the age old problem of getting a donkey to move. How is it done? Whack it or threaten to whack it with a stick (immediate or anticipated pain)? Put a carrot out in front of it (immediate or anticipated pleasure)? Help it realize it is not a donkey at all but a pathologically positive racehorse, born to run – and help it morph into Pegasus, the Pathologically Positive flying Palomino Pony!

When that happens, we can lose the stick, and the carrot. Achievement is imbedded in his psyche. Pegasus simply has to fly.

Thus it is with Pegasus, thus it is with us. Pathologically positive people get clear about who they really are and their purpose on this planet. They speak their energy forward with constructive language, and thereby propel themselves into flying high.

Chapter Twenty One

Your Human Treasury
Nobody Gets Out of This Alive

Death is more universal than life.
Everyone dies but not everyone lives.
~ A. Sachs

A group of brilliant scientists finally discovers how to create human life and excitedly brag about this amazing accomplishment. While they are patting each other on the back, God suddenly appears in their midst. He congratulates them on their great accomplishment and asks them to kindly demonstrate their process.

After taking a moment to get over the shock of the divine visitor appearing to them so suddenly, the scientists agree to give God a little demonstration of their scientific process of creating life.

They explain to God that they actually use a similar method to what they believe He, Himself, used. With common elements, and a high voltage blast of electricity, they will literally create a human being from the dust of the earth.

The scientists start up their generator and, while the voltage builds to the level necessary for their creation demonstration, they bring in a small wheelbarrow of dirt from a neighboring vacant lot.

God interrupts their scientific show and tell.

"Hold on, boys. Get your own dirt!"

Everything has a source, a starting place. Every recipe has ingredients. All ingredients have an origin. All original recipes are therefore not original – except in the way we creatively combine the ingredients.

Some people are convinced that money will solve their problems. Yes, money is indeed a useful tool, so let's get some. Where is the money? It is in the pockets of other people. All of the money in the world is owned by people.

Some think knowledge will solve their problems. Knowledge is power, so let's get some knowledge. Where is the knowledge? In the brains or recorded thoughts of other people. All current knowledge is known by people.

If the money and knowledge are possessed by people, then the solution to our problems must be people. Problems are solved through people – through relationship, conversation, corroboration.

It is people we really need in order to solve our problems.

The most successful companies and businesses understand that their greatest asset is their people. When businesses take care of their people the businesses and their people thrive. When they don't take care of this incredibly valuable resource, they lose it. Fast. People leave; or worse, they stick around, become passively not present, and stop working even more than when they weren't working before. The business falters and fails.

One of the first and fundamental principles of building and maintaining a great business is, as Jim Collins puts it in his book *Good to Great*, to get the right people on board. Having the right people on board, who possess the right set of skills and knowledge and with the right attitude about their work and their company's vision and its mission, is the fundamental formula for success through people. In his preceding book, *Built to Last,* he suggests that your employees are more important even than your customers.

If this is true, then the very problems you are facing right now as you read this book can be solved through your human treasury. Most don't fully appreciate the vast, deep, rich source of solutions and opportunities that this human treasury represents.

My friend, Chad Hymas, has built an impressive speaking business. He presented the keynote address at a conference I attended. Like Art Berg and Steve Brady, Chad is quadriplegic.

During his presentation, Chad invites two members of the audience to come to the stage. Two water bottles sit on the platform. Chad invites his volunteers to take a drink of water from their respective bottles. After the volunteers take a drink, they are instructed to recap the bottles and place them back on the platform.

Chad then instructs the volunteers to take another drink, but as they reach for the bottle he stops them and says, "Wait! This time, you can't use your hands or arms!"

It is pretty funny to watch as these two grown men struggle to get a drink from a water bottle without using their hands or arms. They chase the thing down crawling around on their knees. They then try to grip it between their knees and leverage it somehow to their face. They lie down on the stage and gnaw at the cap with their teeth. There is no observable success. Something as simple as drinking from a small plastic bottle becomes an enormous challenge when deprived of the use of their arms and hands.

What are they to do? How do they get a drink? Must they die of thirst?

One of Chad's volunteers, Blu Robinson, is the founder of *Addict II Athlete*. After wrestling with the bottle for a while, Blu pauses. He notices Chad's assistant seated a little farther back on the stage, and has a brilliant breakthrough. "Would you please help me get a drink of water from this bottle?"

"Sure." Chad's assistant removes the cap and lifts the bottle to Blu's lips.

The other volunteer seems to feel defeated at this point, as if it were a race and he has lost. Chad urges him to continue with the task until he completes it. Even after seeing what Blu did, this second volunteer seems puzzled as to how to solve this problem. Eventually he asks, "Can I do the same thing?"

Chad rolls his eyes in mock exasperation and grants permission to get help from someone else.

Isn't it odd how we see other people succeed, and still feel we lack permission to do the same? Chad's assistant was only one of about six hundred people in the room who were capable and willing to assist. All the volunteers had to do was ask.

But the lesson didn't stop there. Blu Robinson is a close personal friend. A few minutes before the demonstration, Blu was sitting next to me in the audience.

Then he was struggling on the stage with a seemingly impossible task. I watched. I laughed. *And I did nothing to assist.* I let Blu struggle when I could have helped him. Blu didn't ask me for help and I didn't offer. I didn't even think about it. I would have helped if he had asked; but why should he have to ask?

Maybe I suffer from the Lone Ranger Syndrome. Maybe we all do. It seems to be a shared psychosis. Like two-year-olds, we get it into our head that we have to do everything ourselves.

Kirk is a good example. A prominent business leader in our community, Kirk feels guilty in coming to see me about his chronic depression. He has a strong sense of independence. He feels like a failure because he finally has to ask for help. The most honorable and manly thing would be for him to handle this himself. He avoids taking prescribed medication for the same reason. He wants to get well on his own.

He isn't getting better.

I confront Kirk, "Do you *ever* do *anything* by yourself?"

He is a little offended by my question and not quick to answer.

"How about getting dressed in the morning, Kirk; do you do *that* by yourself?"

"Of course I do. That's a stupid question."

"Really? You dress yourself? All by yourself? With what? Do you use clothes you made *yourself* from fabrics you created all by *yourself* from cotton you grew on your own plantation?"

He gets my point.

How many people help *you* get dressed in the morning? How about turning on a light? Did you make the switch? Did you create the light bulb? Where did the electricity come from?

As I draft this chapter, I'm at the Holiday Inn Express in Park City, Utah. I've been here for a few days with Vicki and the kids to get out of town, relax, and enjoy each other for a while. I'm often finished sleeping by five o'clock in the morning. Vicki and the kids, not so much (especially while on vacation). I sneak down to the hotel lobby to get in some writing before everyone wakes up. With laptop at the ready, I look around the beautiful lobby and notice many fine examples of the work other people have done.

The creative minds and talents of literally hundreds, if not thousands, have come together to make it possible for me to sit in comfort in this beautiful leather chair I did not build, with bright steady light emanating from electric bulbs I did not invent, and pleasing decorations I did not fashion.

The elements and ingredients that make up these things already existed in the world, and then were organized into their current state by creative minds and working hands.

The beautiful floor tile was laid by a skilled worker. Someone else had already packaged that tile with other tiles into a bundle the worker opened. Before that, someone had cut or fashioned the stone into a uniformly square shape from raw materials extracted from the earth by other workers using machines they did not themselves create. We should pause in awe every time we notice even the simplest of creations, whether modern or classic.

Thomas, my friend and creative editor, teaches technical presentation skills to European engineers. He is dramatically introduced by Grażyna Słowikowska, his Polish sponsor. He strides to the platform, waves a silk handkerchief and "voila" it becomes a steel magic wand, right in front of the startled engineers' eyes.

"How does magic happen?" Thomas asks, grinning at the stunned engineers. They have no idea. In Europe close up magic is extremely rare. They have never seen such a thing.

"How does magic happen?" Thomas asks again.

They still have no idea.

"Engineering," Thomas responds. "Magic happens because of engineering. Without engineering there is no magic. Without engineering there are no buildings, no watches, no computers, no clothing, no magic, no anything."

How do apple pies happen? Oh, they know the answer to that – they are engineers. "Chemical engineering, of course!"

You know how apple pies happen too. You could make an apple pie from scratch – like Grandma used to make.

However, if you really want to make a truly original apple pie, from scratch, you'll have to invent the apple, the egg, milk, sugar, wheat. In fact you'll have to invent the cow and the chicken and the apple tree.

But *with what* would you create these things? *From what* are they made? The dust of the earth? And would God let you do that – or would he make you go find your own dirt?

All we can really do in creating something new is to reorganize, incorporate, and innovate that which has already been created by other people – people with the knowledge and resources to help us succeed.

I'm not done yet. We are making it too easy. Perhaps creating an original apple pie is even more difficult than simply inventing the ingredients. Carl Sagan, astronomer and writer, said, "If you wish to make an apple pie truly from scratch, you must first invent the universe."

Invent the universe? Wow. That's a pretty tall order just to make a pie – even a really great pie. Grandma didn't actually bake an original pie, but created her unique recipe on what already existed. It sure tasted great, nonetheless.

The very next article of clothing you put on, or product or tool you use, stop for a moment and see if you can determine how many people created, marketed, shipped, customized, sold the item, and instructed you in its use.

You didn't always know how to tie your own shoes, right?

And what about those who help you make it through another day, with or without medication? Make a list of everyone who comes to mind – everyone you know – mere acquaintances as well as people who are close to you. Please include my name. Because you are reading my book, I am now part of your human treasury. Oh, and add my wife's name, and my children, and my associates and friends, and my edit team of thirty very intelligent creative people from all around this wonderful world of ours. They are all a part of my human treasury – and now they are a part of yours.

You are unlikely to ever get to the end of your list. One name triggers another and you realize you cannot ever list all the people who contribute to your success. You will also realize that each of the people on your human treasury list has a human treasury of their own – their family, friends, associates, teachers, mentors, etc. This infinitely interlocked human treasury is what gives us the incredibly rich life we love.

Imagine your list as you now consider your most vexing problem. With this problem in mind, do you now feel alone? Who on your list is most likely to know something or someone that could be a possible solution for that problem?

The solution to your problem is likely just a relationship away. Our success, financial, physical, emotional, even spiritual success depends to a very great extent on establishing and maintaining successful relationships with others.

In the end, at the end (and beyond), nothing else seems to matter quite as much.

Shawn Warenski owns and operates a funeral home. Since I met Shawn as a guest on my show only a few years ago, we have had so far two mutual clients. People appreciate visiting with me, but they are just dying to see Shawn.

You might be wondering why I had an undertaker as a guest on my show, Live on Purpose Radio.[10] The title of our episode was, "Understanding Death: A License to Live." At one point on the show Shawn quoted A. Sachs, "Death is more universal than life. Everyone dies, but not everyone lives."

As we come to terms with the fact that we are indeed mortal, and realize we have — quite literally — a deadline, it changes our perspective about life. It is said that the only sure things in life are death and taxes. We know people who can avoid taxes — but we don't know anyone who can evade death.

Among the most common of fears is the fear of death. It may not be our greatest fear, but its close. Actually, *The Book of Lists* puts the fear of public speaking at the top of the list. Comedian Jay Leno suggests that at a funeral, the person asked to give the eulogy would likely rather be in the casket. Funny — and technically true.

So, why is it that something as universal and certain as death would be feared by so many people? Perhaps it is because even though we can be certain about death, it is not so clear to us what happens afterwards. Most people believe in some kind of continuing existence after death, and most faiths are centered about answering this question so we can put life and death into proper context.

I have several friends who sell life insurance. It is always a little comical to me when people talk about their reasons for buying life insurance. Often they will say something like, "I want to make sure my family has what they need in case I die." What do they mean, "...*in case* I die?"

Whatever our beliefs are about what happens after death, we have to come to terms with the fact that we will all die. This puts a finish line on this life, regardless of what happens

---

[10] www.liveonpurposeradio.com/2011/11/17/understanding-death-a-license-to-live/

afterward. When we are done with this one, we are done — and on to whatever comes next.

My son, Adam, is an avid runner. I have observed in his track meets that runners behave very differently depending on their understanding of where the finish line is. Sprinters get down in the blocks prior to the start, explode into a full run with the gun, and continue at top speed for the entire distance. Long distance runners stand in a group at the start and pace themselves through their race.

A purpose driven life is one in which we know there is a finish line — a deadline. We don't typically get to know when or where that will be. Randy Pausch found out what his deadline was. Randy found out that terminal cancer would end his life in just a few months. In his book, *The Last Lecture*, Randy sprinted to the finish by sharing life's most important lessons for his children to keep forever. He inspired millions in the process.

If we knew our own deadline, would we run differently? Would we really try to run on our own, or would we appreciate the contribution of others? How much more might we focus on our key relationships?

Funerals are a good time and place to ponder what's really important. A few years ago, my grandfather passed away. Dad approached my brother and me after the graveside service. He stood between us with an arm around each of us. He called our attention to the crowd of friends and family visiting and milling about and said, "*This* was your grandfather's treasure."

Of what worth was Grandpa's posterity?

A friend of mine met a stranger on a train. The stranger related a personal story which fundamentally altered my friend's thinking and consequently boosted his career to a higher level.

Of what worth was that stranger on the train?

No man is an island, entire of itself; every man is a piece of the continent, a part of the main. If a clod be washed away by the sea,

Europe is the less, as well as if a promontory were, as well as if a manor of thy friend's or of thine own were: any man's death diminishes me, because I am involved in mankind, and therefore never send to know for whom the bells tolls; it tolls for thee.
~ John Donne 1572-1631

No man is an Iland, intire of it selfe; every man is a peece of the Continent, a part of the maine; if a Clod bee washed away by the Sea, Europe is the lesse, as well as if a Promontorie were, as well as if a Mannor of thy friends or of thine owne were; any mans death diminishes me, because I am involved in Mankinde; And therefore never send to know for whom the bell tolls; It tolls for thee. [Donne's original spelling and punctuation.]

Life can change miraculously in a moment's meeting of someone you may never see again – or who may become your next best friend. Grandpa's posterity was his prosperity. People, and the knowledge and skills they possess, represent the solutions to all of life's problems. Every relationship is more precious than rubies.

I have very much enjoyed the process of writing this book. It's my own original book, copyrighted by me so no one can steal my brilliant ideas. But where did those brilliant ideas come from? Mostly from someone else. Parents, teachers, professors, speakers, other authors, my humble but brilliant editor (who added that line when I wasn't looking).

"Don't worry about people stealing your ideas," says IBM computer engineer, Howard Aiken, "If your ideas are any good, you'll have to ram them down people's throats."

The composer Lukas Foss put it this way, "That is why the analogy of stealing does not work. With a thief, we want to know how much money he stole, and from whom. With the artist it is not how much he took and from whom, but what he did with it."

We take what already exists and build on it with our own creative energy, giving proper credit to whomever wrote the original thought even as we give reverence to the One who created the original apple tree.

I love to brag about my ideas, because none of them are mine. Or was it Bob Proctor who said that? I wonder where he got the idea.

So go, read, observe, watch, learn, absorb. Then write your "own" thoughts, create your "own" wonderful recipe to succeed in business, bake an apple pie from scratch, giving proper credit to your human treasury from whose "original" materials you drew your recipe for success.

CHAPTER TWENTY ONE

Chapter Twenty Two

Life is a Game
Let's Play

Our problem isn't dreaming the impossible dream; our problem is thinking we are supposed to reach the impossible destination.
We are not.
~ Paul H. Jenkins, Ph.D.

We start out in life as children who know how to play games and have fun. Then we grow up, stop playing, and life isn't fun anymore.

Life is a game. Games are meant to be fun. If we are not having fun, are we playing the game wrong? With *Pathological Positivity*, we know we are doing it right when we are having fun. With *Pathological Positivity*, even tough challenges can be fun.

Imagine that our objective is to run between rows of cheering fans, down a track to a finish line marked by a ribbon stretched across the way. We have a destination, and a mission to get there as fast as we can. That's doable. That's fun.

What if our objective is to run to the horizon as fast as we can? That's not so much fun. The horizon is not a place. It is a tool of thinking, a psychological construct, a concept. It doesn't physically exist. No matter how fast or far we run, we will never get there. It isn't a destination. It's impossible, not doable, frustrating. Running to the horizon is zero fun.

When we think our goal or objective is to actually reach implausible or impossible destinations, we are playing a game we cannot win. That is no fun. It is an exhausting, endless ordeal. We can never win. We are left feeling frustrated, inadequate, overwhelmed, exhausted, hopeless, failed.

Our problem isn't dreaming the impossible dream; our problem is thinking we are supposed to actually *reach* the impossible destination.

We are not.

It takes light from Polaris (the North Star) over four centuries to reach earth. It would certainly take a lot longer than that for *us* to reach Polaris.

Polaris doesn't give us much light, and it is too far away to visit. It is not a legitimate vacation destination. So, what good is Polaris to us?

We can never reach the horizon either. So, what good is the horizon to us?

Perfection is like Polaris or the horizon. All three are unreachable. They aren't supposed to be reachable. They are directional standards, measures, benchmarks, ideals. We don't intend to, nor are we intended to, actually get there. Like Polaris, perfection is not a destination. Like the horizon, perfection is not even a real place or position. It would be inappropriate to hold ourselves accountable to be something or someplace that doesn't actually exist.

The horizon is a useful concept when we use it for the right purpose. When our vacation cruise ship sets sail for the horizon, for example, the objective of the cruise is not to arrive at the horizon. We just go that direction and enjoy the trip.

Like Polaris and the horizon, however, the concept of perfection and impossible dreams help us navigate our world by taking us in productive directions. Our outcomes are, therefore, much better than they ever would have been without the standard of perfection that drew us forward.

When I take boy scouts into the wilderness to teach them how to use a compass, we use the horizon for this purpose. If I want the boys to go southeast for twenty paces, I have them find southeast on their compass and get themselves pointed in that direction. They then look to the horizon and find a landmark such as a tall tree, a telephone pole, a mountain peak, or some other prominent, visible standard in that direction to move toward. I don't intend for them to go *to* that standard, I want them to go *toward* it.

At night, we use Polaris. A sparkling unreachable point of light that guides us through the darkness. No way are they going to reach that impossible star. A celestial checkpoint, like a landmark, identifies direction, not destination.

What happens to our feelings when we use an impossible standard for inspiration and direction, but not as an absolute goal? We feel inspired to move *toward* the ideal and advance to a better position in our quest. That feels good. When we know we are moving *toward*, not *to*, an ideal or perfect standard, we have fun. We achieve *The Feeling*. It works. We win!

Nothing in our world is perfect. As we discussed in chapter five, we can always imagine something better than what is. Like the horizon, perfection is a concept or mental tool. Our mental picture of something more perfect is our Polaris to illuminate direction, not evidence of our inadequacy.

It is for creation of what could be, not evaluation of what is.

If perfection is a guide, a valid inspiration, how much imperfection can we tolerate – and still have *The Feeling*?

My brother, Brian, is an engineer. He works with precision equipment. Brian introduced me to the concept of "tolerances." In engineering, a tolerance is not only how close to perfection we need to be for a project to work, it is also an acknowledgement that we know our creation can't be perfect.

How much tolerance do we have for imperfection in ourselves and others? It better be a fair amount, or we'll never get anything done!

What if a carpenter were asked to cut something *exactly* one inch? Would that be any different from asking him to run to the horizon? How would he cut the material to *exactly* one inch? The only thing he could do is measure it against something else (usually his measuring tape) to determine where to cut. If he draws a line at the one inch mark with a lead pencil, as carpenters usually do, where does he make his cut? Under a microscope, the line looks as wide as a freeway. Which part of that wide black line is one inch?

The line on his measuring tape, upon which he gauged where to make the line with his pencil, is also a freeway under the microscope.

Even with imperfect measures and standards, we can build a perfectly beautiful home

I recently got a personal tour of the Blendtec factory from Tom Dickson, inventor of the amazing Blendtec blenders featured in the viral YouTube "Will It Blend" series.[11] Tom describes the tight tolerances required to make the parts for these precision machines. As great as these blenders are, Tom knows they are not perfect. How far from perfect can something be and still work? That is a "tolerance."

Those who judge themselves based on a standard of perfection — with no tolerance allowance — create feelings of inadequacy, frustration, hopelessness, depression. There is always another dollar to earn, another toy to accumulate, additional praise to seek, more power to control, and absolutely, positively zero tolerance for dumb mistakes. In the pursuit of perfection, we must make certain nothing bad, painful, or uncomfortable ever happens to us — and that we never make mistakes.

And we don't achieve a dang thing.

We waste and wear out our lives pursuing unreachable horizons, and end up feeling exhausted, empty, incomplete, inadequate. Our goal is still impossible and as far away as Polaris.

We can never win if perfection is the definition of "winning."

In the movie, *Finding Nemo*, Marlin tells Dory about his son, Nemo. Marlin is blaming and beating himself up for having lost Nemo.

---

[11] www.willitblend.com

Marlin:	I promised I'd never let anything happen to him.
Dory:	Hmm. That's a funny thing to promise.
Marlin:	What?
Dory:	Well, you can't never let anything happen to him. Then nothing would ever happen to him. Not much fun for little Harpo (Dory can never seem to remember Nemo's name).

So if the objective is not to reach the horizon, pitch a tent on Polaris, and let nothing bad happen along the way, then what is the purpose of the game? It is an "impossible purpose." Therefore, it has no practical purpose at all.

The real object of the game of life is as obvious as the shirt on your back. Our real purpose is to achieve *The Feeling* by living the life we love. That is totally do-able.

If we are not having fun, we're doing it wrong. Consider how fundamental this objective is. In chapter three we illuminated *The Feeling* as the obvious, but often unnoticed purpose behind our choices and actions.

Why do you go to work?
"To earn money."

Why?
"So I can support my family, of course."

Why do you want to support your family?
"So we can have a good life, of course."

Why do you want a good life?
"Huh? So we can be happy, of course. Isn't that obvious?"

Yes, of course. *The Feeling.*

This line of questioning (inspired by two-year olds) is increasingly unnecessary as the fundamental purpose becomes increasingly obvious. We do what we do in order to gain *The Feeling*. To gain *The Feeling* for ourselves and do what we can so others around us can also enjoy *The Feeling*.

The goal is always some form of joy, happiness, satisfaction, fun, for us and others. We will even deny ourselves *The Feeling* to let others have *The Feeling*. Doing this actually gives us *The Feeling* – so we do it.

We've known this for quite some time. Ancient text written around 600 BC has been translated to read, "...men are, that they might have joy."[12] Call it joy, happiness, meaning, the very reason for existence, the purpose behind everything that we do, is to experience more of *The Feeling*.

Another philosopher proposed around 200 BC, "Happiness is the absence of the striving for happiness."[13] We win when we create *The Feeling*. That does not come from *trying* to be happy, but choosing to be so regardless of our circumstances.

We choose to love, serve, learn, achieve meaning, live on purpose the life we love. We win the game by being happy.

---

[12]Lehi (A prophet mentioned in *The Book of Mormon*, 2 Nephi 2:25, about 588 BC)

[13]Chuang Tzu (One of China's early interpreters of Taoism, 389-286 BC)

Chapter Twenty Three

Do It Now
*There is No Time **But** the Present*

Through intentional repeated practice of Pathological Positivity, a new default is set, and our conditioned response becomes one of habitual positivity. We live on purpose, meaning that we have a purpose and we do it intentionally.
~ Paul H. Jenkins, Ph.D.

We keep our commitments. We create stories. We do one or the other – usually not both.

If we don't keep our commitments, we tell stories that justify why we didn't. These stories may be true, interesting, compelling, or intriguing.

They are stories, nevertheless.

A couple shows up twenty minutes late for their appointment. They bustle through the door and launch into their story before they even sit down. Their story is an apologetic, compelling tale of construction delays, game-day traffic, accidents on the freeway...

It's a great story.

It might even be true.

It is a story nonetheless.

Why did they feel compelled to tell their story before even settling on the couch? Because they did not keep their commitment to be on time for their appointment. Had they kept their commitment, the story would not have been necessary. The story would never have been told (or created) in the first place.

"But," you may protest in their defense, "They can't control the traffic. They did everything they could to be there on time. They were just explaining why it is not their *fault* they were late."

Yes, you are right — and the story is still a story.

The stories we create about *why* we don't keep commitments are there to help us feel less guilty about not keeping them, and perhaps to convince others that we are still good people and don't deserve the consequences that come with not keeping commitments.

But the consequences come nevertheless.

Early in my career, I ran a multi-family therapy group for teens and their parents. These teens had been referred to our program through the juvenile court. They always had great stories with colorful reasons why they were there.

One evening Brittany rushes into our group session about a half hour late. Her mom files in behind her. Brittany interrupts the flow of the group to announce that she is ready to advance to the next level — which carries with it additional privileges. She asks the group to approve her advancement.

The group is slow to respond to her request. Actually, they sit and stare at her as if she is a visitor from outer space.

I ask her if she really thinks her request for advancement is appropriate considering that she has not kept her commitment to be on time for the group. Brittany retorts, "Hey, I would have been on time, but Mom got off work late and we couldn't get here till now."

Someone in group meekly suggests that her request for advancement be denied because she didn't keep her commitment to be at all group meetings on time.

Brittany blows her cork. "What? Why? Deny me why? Because I'm late? That's not fair. You're not listening to me. The only reason I was late is because Mom got off work late! That's not my fault!"

Some members of the group rally in sympathetic support for Brittany's position. She does, after all, have a believable story. This triggers discussion about whether we should let her advance and not hold her accountable for keeping her commitment to be on time.

In analyzing this situation properly, we need a little background information.

Brittany is in our program because the juvenile court identified her as being "ungovernable." She and her mother are in my program, by order of the Court, to establish more functional and responsible patterns, such as Brittany's attending school rather than roaming around causing mischief.

Today, her mother called Brittany to let her know she would be late getting home from work. Knowing her mother would be unable to get off work on time to make the group, Brittany could have walked the distance from her home to my office and kept her commitment to herself and the group by being on time. But she chose not to. Instead she chose to create a story about how it was her mother's fault that she was late.

Here are a couple more helpful facts. Brittany was sent to our program after being arrested for committing a few minor crimes – in Las Vegas. Las Vegas is three hundred miles from her home. Brittany's home is less than three miles from my office.

What was Brittany asking the group to believe? That she could find her way to Las Vegas for a little outlaw fun, but not walk three miles down the road to be on time for our group session?

Yes, she was denied her request for advancement.

What if your friend asks you if you have read the draft of her short story that you agreed to review for her and send right back? Your response might be, "Oh, I'm sorry, I've been so busy this week I haven't had time to get to that yet."

This is a story – and it's not even a true story. She did have time. The truth would sound more like, "I had other things to do this week that were more important to me than reading your story." But that would sound rude, so to make it more palatable, we make up the story about not having time to do what we promised.

"I didn't have time" is a variation of "the dog ate my homework," "the devil made me do it," or "it is Mom's fault." None of them are true. The dog did not eat your homework, it is not the devil's fault or your parent's and, yes, you do have time.

What if I were to offer you eighty-six thousand four hundred dollars, would you accept it? There is, of course, a catch. You have to spend it *all*. Not only that, but you have to spend it all *today*.

I am sure you would gladly accept the challenge – and you would do your best to spend it all – my kids would have no problem doing it.

Whether you spend it all or not today, what if I offered you an additional and equal amount tomorrow with the same conditions? The next day you get the same deal, and the next, and the next.

Would you like that?

This is exactly the deal we get with our time. We get twenty four hours. This equates to eighty-six thousand four hundred seconds today. The catch is, we have to spend it all *today*. We lose what we don't use. But don't worry, there is another eighty-six thousand plus coming tomorrow, and the next day, and every day after that. Eighty-six thousand four hundred shiny new seconds automatically deposited in our account at midnight every night after the previous day's balance is zeroed out.

This is the same deal for you, for me, for the poor family down the street, and for the gazillionaire you heard about on *Lifestyles of the Rich and Famous*.

How we spend our time is our choice, but we have to spend it now. Time cannot be saved, stored, shared, bought, multiplied, or even managed. "Buying time" or "managing your time" are misnomers. The only thing we can do with time is spend it or waste it (although wasting time is a way of spending it – on things that have little or no value).

Time is the most constantly renewable resource in the universe. We *do* have time. We have all the time we can spend today; then we get more tomorrow.

The only time we can do anything is *now*. We have developed habits of saying that there is always later, but this isn't quite accurate. When we actually do it is now. Time keeps up with us. We can't get ahead of it. It is always now. This realization makes a big difference as we talk to ourselves about time and how we use our time.

World class leadership trainer, Ron Zeller, teaches the principle of doing things now. This feels a bit overwhelming when we think of all of the things we want to do or are required of us. To do all of those things *right now* is not possible. But *now* is the only time we can do anything, so how can we do everything now without getting overwhelmed?

For Ron, "now" is defined as having a start time, an end time, and a specific activity between those two endpoints. Our calendar or day planner is a tool to line up our "now's." I have created "now's" for next week. Some of my "now's" will be spent with clients, either in the office or from the speaker's platform. During a client "now," the only thing I will be spending my time on is thinking about and having conversations with that particular client. I work with them to create and live the life they love, through the art and science of *Pathological Positivity.*

I can't have interactions and conversations with clients "later" because "later" never gets here. Only "now" shows up on my watch and calendar. The particular time and date I see on my watch tell me which "now" I am in.

This is not a time management technique (remember, you can't manage time) it is a *self* management technique. It is a method of creating a consciousness for living in the now. It is a way of looking at what appears to be an overwhelming bunch of stuff to do and making a conscious choice about what we will do about it, to it, with it. It is a way to be honest and truthful with ourselves about what we declare to be important or valuable. We take respons*ability* for keeping commitments by turning "I should do that" or "Someday I will…" into a calendar item on our list of "now's."

Or we just do it.

Now.

Create a habit of doing things now, rather than pushing them off to some undefined "later." Ask, "Is this potential use of my time really something that adds value?" If it does not, then it doesn't qualify for a "now." It if does add value, we create a "now." Do it now.

Ron's concept of "now" is reassuring. Once we give ourselves a now when our commitment will be fulfilled, we release the pressure and guilt of carrying around un-kept commitments. We can use our storytelling talents in more productive ways, like spicing up bedtime for our adorable kids, grandkids, nieces, nephews.

Is that a great idea?

So, let's do it.

Now.

Chapter Twenty Four

Live On Purpose
Create and Live the Life You Love

*Joy is what happens to us when we allow ourselves to
recognize how good things really are.*
~Marianne Williamson

My wife reads the end of the book first. Whether novels or mystery, she simply must know how the book turns out before she will invest her time in reading it. So, for my dear Vicki, here is the summary to read first. For those of us who are more traditional in the way we read a book, here it is to wrap up what you just read.

We have examined different elements of two processes: The first process is evaluation of *what is*. The second process is creation of *what is to be*.

We do both – constantly. Often at the same time. It is in our very nature to do so. We evaluate our circumstances, our lives, ourselves, and imagine how it could be different.

One of the purposes of this book is to inspire metacognition, and to illuminate the obvious fact that we constantly evaluate and create. As we think about our engagement in these two processes, we are in position to do both on purpose with full awareness that we are doing it.

As we evaluate *what is* we intentionally find the good in it. Doing so brings *The Feeling* now – even when *what is* normally would seem bad. We honestly say *what is* is good because, for one thing, we can always imagine something worse, thereby making *what is* look good by comparison.

In addition, we now seek and find the good in or about the situation itself. We don't find good *in spite of* the situation or find good that *comes out of* the situation; rather, we find that the situation, *the so-called disaster itself,* is good.

Because of this perception that everything is (or can be) considered good, we feel gratitude even in the midst of apparent disaster.

We then create *what is to be*.

Though we realize there is good in the disaster, we don't stay in the disaster. We imagine something better, not for the purpose of beating ourselves up for not having done or become that better thing, but to guide our efforts in causing or creating a better *what is to be*.

We also create this better *what is to be* even when there is no disaster, and things are just fine,

Our ability to constantly imagine something greater than *what is,* no matter how great *what is* may be, helps us make this constant upgrade, and the life we love, possible.

We feel creative discontent. We imagine and create something better. Life is good. Appreciating the good in *what is,* then anticipating an even greater good in *what is to be* brings *The Feeling* immediately.

As we evaluate and create, *constructively and intentionally*, life makes more sense. We feel in control, like agents rather than victims, even in tough situations. Rather than mindlessly meddling in messes — and making them messier — we direct our creative power toward the productive and beautiful. We build things of intrinsic worth and beauty. We acknowledge the value in *what is* and create new value moving forward for ourselves and others.

The creation process anticipates, requires, and is initiated by the first step, discontent.

Discontent

Discontent strikes. It might be in the form of pain, dissatisfaction, hunger, yearning, wishing, hoping, or just imagining that things could be better because we have an attitude of continual improvement.

It is easy to misinterpret (evaluate) discontent as evidence that *what is* is bad. But that would be like judging the foundation as bad because the building isn't yet complete.

Creators must experience discontent in order to know what and how to create. Discontent identifies the problems and challenges that create new opportunities (propportunities). Thus, discontent is a good thing.

Discontent   Choice

Discontent triggers choice. Whether positively or negatively, constructively or destructively, actively or passively, we choose what we will do with our discontent in evaluation and creation.

In the process, we also choose whether to view or perceive our circumstances in victim mode or agent mode. In victim mode, we recycle our discontent. We churn it around, enhancing our story about why life stinks. "Why me? Why this? Why now?" In agent mode we appreciate and seek the opportunities present in problems. We use discontent to generate, ask, and answer better questions. "Why *not* me? Why *not* this? If not this, then what?"

CHAPTER TWENTY FOUR

Discontent   Choice   Question

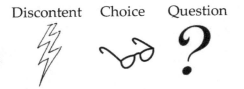

We question. Our positive choice to move forward in agent mode leads us to ask positive, constructive questions. This might take more effort than we anticipate, but not as much as we fear. As we ask and answer the right questions, and listen to or come up with constructive answers, we power up the creation process and move naturally into the next step, planning for our success.

Discontent   Choice   Question   Plan

We plan. Things don't just magically pop into existence, they are planned. Everything that is intentionally created exists first as an idea. Like a seed, the thought of what is needed, desired, wanted, is planted – usually as a result of a *propportunity* formerly known as a *problem*.

Constructive questions about why that problem exists lead to rational answers and constructive planning of upgrades to solve the problem and thereby celebrate the propportunity. Then we go to work to bring the plan to fruition in the form of a practical, mechanical, medical, architectural, artistic, creative solution.

Discontent Choice Question Plan Work

We get to work. We cannot create or destroy matter — we just change its form. In physics, the power by which we do this is *transference of energy* or *force*. We common folk usually call it work.

Philosophers love to contemplate it.

Successful people love to do it.

Images we create in our minds as we plan become templates that guide the work that changes our ideas and raw materials into something that looks like those template images. This is not only true of physical creations, it is also true of intangible creations like attitudes, relationships, careers; all of which manifest in reality because of our work and the work of others. Work is the means to the miracle.

Discontent Choice Question Plan Work Manifest

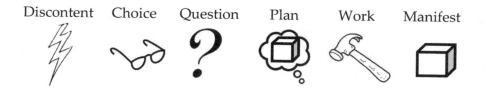

We satisfy our discontent by manifesting that which we have chosen to create. We face problems and work constructively on solutions. Our thoughts and ideas therefore, and thereby, manifest as reality.

We take control of our lives by intentionally steering the process from evaluation to creation. A pathologically positive approach exponentially enhances this process of evaluation and creation. We start by declaring *what is* — whatever that may be —

to be good. Not potentially good, but immediately good — whether or not we clearly see yet *why* it is good.

When we perceive *what is* as good, we immediately experience success, joy, peace, happiness, acceptance, gratitude, a sense of meaning; in other words, *The Feeling*.

After we evaluate *what is*, we create *what is to be*. We do it intentionally. As we imagine an even better *what is to be*, we experience more of *The Feeling*.

The Feeling releases energy and creates focus which puts us in position to further upgrade *what is*. As we upgrade, we enjoy more of *The Feeling*. As we enjoy *The Feeling*, we visualize, plan, and create further upgrades. This causes us to immediately experience *even more* of *The Feeling*. We feel positive anticipation, energy, confidence, excitement and even greater success in a perpetual pattern of *Pathological Positivity*.

We recognize, honor, celebrate, and drive this process intentionally. We are filled with *The Feeling* of success. We are therefore filled with success — "success-full." Life is good. And, in a continuing upward spiral, it gets continually better.

We therefore and thereby live on purpose. We have fun. We create and live the life we love through the applied science of *Pathological Positivity*.

℞

Your *Pathological Positivity* prescription
to create, and live on purpose,
the healthy, happy, successful life you love.

When people read a book they are typically looking for
entertainment or ideas. They do not necessarily intend
do anything about those ideas. Me too. I love to be
entertained. I love to think about and talk about new ideas.

My life changes when I actually *do something* about those
ideas. But that doesn't usually happen. Why? Because the ideas
are complex or difficult? Because they present a break in my
comfortable routine? Maybe they are too new or challenging or
controversial to simply adopt without serious processing,
planning, preparation.

That's why this book is different.
It is intended to be applied.
It is *designed* to be applied.

The principles in this book will not be proven through
debate. They are proven in the lives of those who try them. I,
therefore, invite *you* to try taking the *Pathological Positivity*
prescription.

You don't have to be comfortable with the idea. You don't
have to like it. You don't have to believe it will work. You
simply try it. The prescription is simple, easy, doable, *and will
work, even through our own resistance.* It will work a dramatic change

in your life. It will make you better, feel better, do better – at everything worth doing – and you will experience amazingly enhanced rewards for your efforts.

Are you feeling resistance? That's okay. This prescription will nudge you out of your comfort zone a bit. That's good. It means you are on the right track.

Notice the resistance, and take your medicine anyway. Fill the *Pathological Positivity* prescription, take as directed, and simply remain open to the possibility that it will improve your life.

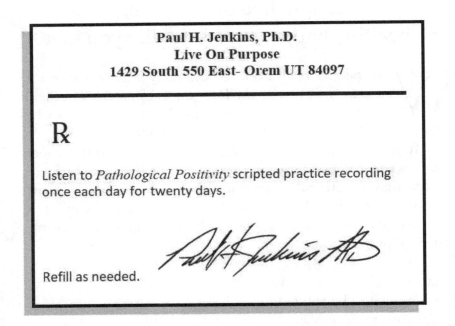

Paul H. Jenkins, Ph.D.
Live On Purpose
1429 South 550 East- Orem UT 84097

R

Listen to *Pathological Positivity* scripted practice recording once each day for twenty days.

Refill as needed.

Step One – Fill Your Prescription.

1.1   Prepare an audio recording of the *Pathological Positivity* Script that follows these instructions. This takes about an hour. If now is not the right time for you to do this, get out your calendar right now and schedule the right time within the next four days. Make an appointment with yourself to actually do this. Keep your appointment!

1.2 Obtain a device to record your voice. Any recording/ playback device that is easy and convenient for you to use will work for this prescription. It could be your phone, tablet, computer, digital recorder, even an old fashioned tape recorder.

1.3 Obtain some classical music.[14] Handel, Mozart, or another classical composer you like. Cue up the music to play in the background as you make your recording.

1.4 Practice reading the *Pathological Positivity* script (found immediately after these instructions) out loud a few times to prepare for the recording. This will make the wording more familiar and improve the flow. Read it as naturally as possible, yet with feeling and emphasis.

1.5 Find a quiet place with your equipment where you can be undisturbed for the recording.

1.6 Start the music and the recording device and record, in your own voice, the *Pathological Positivity* script you just rehearsed. Quality of performance is not the key issue here. The important thing is to record it in your own voice with the music playing in the background. Ann Webb, of Ideal LifeVision explains that your own voice is your most believable voice. Your own voice together with the effect of the music in the background create a powerful personalized tool that installs these ideas into your subconscious.

1.7 In a pinch, you may use my voice instead – although your own voice will be much more powerful and convincing to your subconscious. Still, it is better to feed this information to your mind than to bypass it because

---

[14]Technique inspired by Ann Webb. www.IdealLifeVision.com

it is challenging to make your own recording. An MP3 version of my voicing of the script for you can be obtained (no cost) through:

https://DrPaulJenkins.info/Prescription

Step Two – Take Your Prescription.

2.1   Decide the time and place that works best for you to listen to your recording every day. This could be as you wake up, in the bathroom as you get ready for your day, while you exercise, in your car, over lunch, just before bed.

2.2   Build in systems to make sure you take your prescription every day for twenty days. Set yourself up to succeed by putting devices or reminders in place so you trust yourself to take it. A note on your mirror, this book or the playback device on the seat of your car, a recurring appointment in your calendar, a marble in your shoe, a rock on your pillow, a nagging spouse, an alarm that automatically plays your recording to wake you up in the morning, anything that prompts the action and assures its regular daily completion.

Pathological Positivity Script
Record this declaration in your own voice.
Listen to it *every* day for twenty days.[15]

I love my life. I am happy and grateful for what is, and eagerly anticipate even better things to come. Yesterday I learned and experienced exactly what I need to succeed at an even greater level today and tomorrow.

Discontent is a powerful indicator of opportunity. I welcome discontent as a necessary foundation for creativity and success. I notice and accept all of my feelings, whether they are pleasant or not. I am always right about how I feel because my feelings are consistent with my current perceptions and beliefs. I recognize, however, that facts are likely different than what I see. Pain is a gift. Problems are opportunities. My feelings change about these things as my perceptions evolve and improve.

I am a creator, builder, producer. I choose and embody gratitude, compassion, respons*ability*. I *choose* to see the good in all experiences. I *choose* to see good in all people. I predict positive outcomes. I assume the best. I choose *Pathological Positivity* as my governing position toward people and all of life's challenges and opportunities.

I find constructive possibilities in *every* experience. I ask probing questions about circumstances. My questions are actually questions, not statements disguised as questions. I stay in the

---

[15] If it feels too complicated to actually use the method I suggest, simply read this script out loud every day. Read with feeling and conviction. Whatever way we take this prescription, it will work – provided we take it every day as prescribed.

question and continue to observe all that goes on around me, until the answer becomes clear and the best course of action presents itself.

I focus thought and language on desired results. I visualize, speak, hear my intended outcomes as if they already exist. I frame my thoughts and my speech around what I have, what I want, and what I can do, not the negative opposites. My objectives are noble, worthwhile, clear, detailed. I accept that I have the power and resources to make them real. I acknowledge the contributions of others toward my success.

I feel empathy and compassion for others who experience discontent. I build, lift, bless, serve, contribute, produce. I create value and help others realize their dreams. My contributions are meaningful, valuable, significant. I apply diligent daily effort in creating desired outcomes. I do what I love, for those who love what I do. No matter what happens, I move forward every day happy and enthused for the difference I make in this world.

I am profoundly grateful for my abundant life and the abundance I create in the world.

Acknowledgements

Only authors and their families really know what it takes to create a book. A big shout out to my amazing family for their phenomenal support starting with my Heavenly Father. His greatest blessing to me, along with my life and my mind is my wife, Vicki. She is followed closely by Ryan and Jessica, Adam and Nolle, Brennan and Ashley, Lyndi, three adorable grandkids (so far), my parents, siblings, and extended family.

My edit team, led by the legendary Thomas Cantrell, was absolutely indispensable in this project. Thomas was much more than a creative editor, he became a permanent friend and associate through the process of writing this book and working with me to fine-tune my spoken message. Thomas challenged my thinking in a way that refined this book from the brain dump I handed to him as a first draft, to a unique yet coherent message with global impact.

Our edit team for the first edition includes Rosemarie Woodward (who did the original cover), Heather Clark, Ken Gallacher, Emilia Butler, Brady Giles, Kathie Leany, Lorin Blauer, Cindi Hunter, Jalene Lott, Sydney-Ann Porter, Su Boddie, Rita Kano, Evan Baker, Richard Potter, Johnnie Bobo, Kathryn Thompson, Irene Jones, Grażyna Słowikowska, Charles and Sharon Jenkins, and Charlie Wakamatsu. These good people from all around the world provided critically valuable feedback and input during the editing process. The second edition was influenced by dozens of additional readers and team members.

Dozens of people have impacted the direction and message of this book. Special acknowledgements to Brad Barton, Chad Hymas, Mayor Ralph Becker, Leslie Householder, Kate Adamson, Woody Woodward, Les McGuire, Mark Eaton, Brett Harward, Mary Louise Zeller, Dr. Randy Hyde, Darren Johansen, Craig Rollo, Dr. John Livingstone, Dr. Jason Adams, Jeni Roper, Mike Schlappi, Zhu Qin, Andrew Cengiz, Ryan Bradshaw, Ty Bennett, Andrew Giles, Kirk Weisler, Blu

Robinson, Matt Townsend, Tom Dickson, Camie Rose, Dr. Jeff McGee, Ron Zeller, Shawn Warenski, Steve Brady, Richard Paul Evans, Mark Gungor, Jill Stevens, Jon Gordon, Hyrum Smith, Mark Sanborn, Pam Hansen, Rich Christiansen, Ann Webb, my guests at Live On Purpose Radio, my awesome followers at Live On Purpose TV (YouTube), and my phenomenal friends and colleagues in the National Speakers Association – especially the Mountain West Chapter.

Bibliography

Achor, Shawn. *The Happiness Advantage: The Seven Principles of Positive Psychology That Fuel Success and Performance at Work.* Crown Business. 2010.

Adamson, Kate. *Paralyzed but not Powerless.* Nosmada Press. 2007.

Arthur, Joel. *Paradigms.* HarperBusiness; Reprint Edition. 1993.

Aylesworth, John and Frank Peppiatt. *Hee Haw.* Television comedy/variety show. Directed by Bill Davis and Bob Boatman. Columbia Broadcasting System (CBS) and Gaylord Productions. 1969-1997.

Barton, Brad. *Beyond Illusions: The Magic of Positive Perception.* Executive Books. 2008.

Berg, Art. *The Impossible Just Takes a Little Longer.* William Morrow Paperbacks. 2003.

Burrows, James, Glen Charles, and Les Charles. *Cheers.* Television series. Directed by James Burrows. Produced by Charles/Burrows/Charles Productions in association with Paramount Network Television. Distributed by National Broadcasting Company (NBC). 1982-1993.

Byrne, Rhonda. *The Secret.* Atria Books/Beyond Words. 2006.

Byrne, Rhonda. *The Secret.* DVD. Directed by Drew Heriot, Sean Byrne, Marc Goldenfein, and Damian McLindon. Prime Time Productions and Nine Network Australia. 2007.

Cantrell, Thomas. *Yes Man Theorem.* Downside Up Publishing. 2014.

Clason, George S. *The Richest Man in Babylon.* Signet. 2002.

Cohen, I. Bernard. *Howard Aiken: Portrait of a Computer Pioneer.* The MIT Press. 1999.

Collins, Jim. *Good to Great: Why Some Companies Make the Leap...And Others Don't.* HarperBusiness. 2001.

Collins, Jim, and Jerry I. Porras. *Built to Last: Successful Habits of Visionary Companies.* HarperBusiness. 1994.

Covey, Stephen R. *The 7 Habits of Highly Effective People: Powerful Lessons in Personal Change.* Simon & Schuster; Anniversary Edition edition. 2013.

Crystal, Billy, and David Seltzer. *My Giant.* DVD. Directed by Michael Lehmann. Castle Rock Entertainment and Face Productions. 1998.

Dick, Philip K., and Scott Frank. *Minority Report*. DVD. Directed by Steven Spielberg. Twentieth Century Fox Film Corporation, DreamWorks SKG, and Cruise/Wagner Productions. 2002.

Elliott, Ted, Terry Rossio, Stuart Beattie, and Jay Wolpert. *Pirates of the Caribbean: The Curse of the Black Pearl*. DVD. Directed by Gore Verbinski. Walt Disney Pictures, and Jerry Bruckheimer Films. 2003.

Evans, Richard Paul. *The Spyglass: A Book About Faith*. Simon & Schuster Children's Publishing. 2000.

Frankl, Viktor. *Man's Search for Meaning*. Pocket Books. 1997. Revised updated mass media paperback edition.

Gardner, Pierce, and Peter Hedges. *Dan in Real Life*. DVD. Directed by Peter Hedges. Touchstone Pictures, Focus Features, Jon Shestack Productions. 2007.

Grant, Susannah, Andy Tennant, Rick Parks, and Charles Perrault. *Ever After: A Cinderella Story*. DVD. Directed by Andy Tennant. Twentieth Century Fox Film Corporation. 1998.

Groom, Winston, and Eric Roth. *Forrest Gump*. DVD. Directed by Robert Zemeckis. Paramount Pictures. 1994.

Gungor, Mark. *Laugh Your Way to a Better Marriage: Unlocking the Secrets to Life, Love, and Marriage*. Atria Books and Simon and Schuster Digital Sales Inc. 2008. Kindle edition.

Hansel, Tim. *You Gotta Keep Dancin'*. David C. Cook. 1998. New edition.

Harman, Willis. *An Incomplete Guide to the Future*. W. W. Norton & Company. 1979.

Harward, Brett. *The 5 Laws That Determine All of Life's Outcomes*. FranklinCovey Publishing. 2008. Second edition.

Howes, Ryan. *The definition of Insanity is…* In *Psychology Today, In Therapy* (July 27, 2009). Retrieved from http://www.psychologytoday.com/blog/in-therapy/200907/the-definition-insanity-is. 2009.

Hymas, Chad. *Doing What Must Be Done*. Chad Hymas Communications. 2012.

Jeffers, Susan. *Feel the Fear and Do It Anyway*. Ballantine Books. 2006.

King, Stephen. *On Writing: 10th Anniversary Edition: A Memoir of the Craft*. Scribner. 2010.

Kuhn, Thomas S. *The Structure of Scientific Revolutions*. Chicago: University of Chicago Press, 1970.

Nightingale, Earl. *The Strangest Secret*. Ophelia Madison Press LLC. 2012. Kindle Edition.

Pausch, Randy, and Jeffrey Zaslow. *The Last Lecture*. Hyperion. 2008.

Porter, Eleanor H., and David Swift. *Pollyanna*. DVD. Directed by David Swift. Walt Disney Productions. 1960.

Roberts, Allan, and Doris Fisher. *Into Each Life Some Rain Must Fall*. Audio MP3. Performed by The Ink Spots with Ella Fitzgerald. From the Album Legendary Vocal Groups Vol. 1. Pink Flamingo Records. 2012.

Robertson, Korie, and Robertson family. *Duck Dynasty*. Reality television series. Directed by Hugh Peterson and David Hobbes. Gurney Productions. 2012-2014.

Rowling, J.K., and Steve Kloves. Harry Potter and the Sorcerer's Stone. DVD. Directed by Chris Columbus. Warner Bros., Heyday Films, and 1492 Pictures. 2001.

Rubin, Danny, and Harold Ramis. *Groundhog Day*. DVD. Directed by Harold Ramis. Columbia Pictures Corporation. 1993.

Rubin, Theodore I. *Compassion and Self Hate: An Alternative to Despair*. Touchstone. 1998.

Sachar, Louis. *Holes*. DVD. Directed by Andrew Davis. Walt Disney Pictures, Walden Media, and Chicago Pacific Entertainment. 2003.

Sanborn, Mark. *The Fred Factor: How Passion in Your Work and Life Can Turn the Ordinary into the Extraordinary*. Currency. 2004.

Schlappi, Mike. *Shot Happens*. Brigham Distributing. 2009.

Schulz, Kathryn. "On Being Wrong." TED Talk. Retrieved from http://www.ted.com/talks/kathryn_schulz_on_being_wrong.html. 2011.

Shakespeare, William. *Hamlet*. Waxkeep Publishing. 2013. Kindle edition.

Shenk, David. *The Genius in All of Us: New Insights into Genetics, Talent and IQ*. Anchor Books: a division of Random House, Inc. 2010.

Smith, Adam. *Powers of the Mind*. Random House. 1975.

Smith, Joseph (translator). *The Book of Mormon: Another Testament of Jesus Christ*. The Church of Jesus Christ of Latter-day Saints. 1981.

Stanton, Andrew, Bob Peterson, and David Reynolds. *Finding Nemo*. DVD. Directed by Andrew Stanton and Lee Unkrich. Walt Disney Pictures and Pixar Animation Studios. 2003.

Stevens, Jill. *It's All Good*. Brigham Distributing. 2008.

Stratton, George M. "Some preliminary experiments on vision without inversion of the retinal image." *Psychological Review* 3(6): 611-7. 1896.

Wallechinski, David. Amy Wallace, Ira Basen, and Jane Farrow. *The Book of Lists: The Original Compendium of Curious Information*. Seal Books. 2006. Reprint edition.

Wilkinson, Bruce, David Kopp, and Heather Kopp. The Dream Giver. Multnomah Books. 2003.

Ready for more?

Get a concise summary of Dr. Paul's model for positivity in a pocket-sized mini book!

PortablePositivity.com

About the Author

Dr. Paul Jenkins is a leading expert in the psychology of positivity. With decades of experience as a professional psychologist, Dr. Paul (as he is known to clients and his audiences) is on a mission to increase happiness, profit, engagement, and productivity for organizations and individuals. Listening to Dr. Paul is like having an owner's manual for your brain – one you can actually read, understand, and apply. His clients, readers, and audiences get an iron grip on powerful principles that make an immediate difference in their personal, family, and professional lives.

When this "shrink" isn't shrinking your negativity on YouTube, in a coaching program, or from the microphone, he can be found playing with grandkids, shooting around with a basketball, or making his wife wonder if he will ever grow up.

DrPaulJenkins.com

LiveOnPurposeRadio.com

YouTube.com/LiveOnPurposeTV

About the Editor

Thomas Cantrell's keen intellect and commitment to "practical perfection" clarifies the key message of his clients in both written and spoken presentations. He ruthlessly challenges the standard of common thought; then, through practical application of innovative ideas in his own life, proves them true.

Thomas is driven by passion and commitment to creating positive change world-wide through positive, constructive communication.

You may contact him by e-mail: Tom@TomCantrell.com

PAUL H. JENKINS, PH.D.

LIVE ON PURPOSE

ISBN:
978-0-9904520-5-8